The Essential Collection of PC Questions and Answers

ROB YOUNG

Published by Agora Business Publications

Agora Business Publications LLP
Nesfield House
Broughton Hall Business Park
Skipton
BD23 3AN

Publisher: Victoria Burrill
Author: Rob Young

Phone: 01756 693 180
Fax: 01756 693 196
Email: cs@agorapublications.co.uk
Web: www.agorabusinesspublications.co.uk

ISBN: 978-1-908245-01-4

Agora Business Publications LLP. Nesfield House, Broughton Hall Business Park, Skipton, Yorkshire,
BD23 3AN. Registered in England No. OC323533, VAT No. GB 893 3184 95.

Contents

4. Get to Know Your Hardware – and Start Using It YOUR Way

5. Software Problems Fixed Instantly

6. Solve Windows Error Messages Fast

7. Get Rid of Annoying Email Problems for Optimal Use

8. Microsoft Word Troubleshooting: Create Error Free Stylish Documents with Ease

Introduction

Welcome to *The Essential Collection of PC Questions and Answers!*

Whether you're an absolute beginner or a more-experienced computer user, you're sure to have questions about your PC. A curiosity of computers is that it doesn't matter how much you already know – there always seems to be something waiting just around the corner to catch you out!

For 15 years I've been writing about computers and answering readers' questions about them. Like the organised sort of chap I am, I've kept copies of all these questions and answers because – of course – many questions come up more than once. In fact, some come up over and over again!

In this book, I've gathered my favourite questions and answers, combining those that crop up most frequently with others that cover more unusual and interesting topics – the types of niggling issue we all find ourselves grappling with from time to time but struggle to find an answer for.

As you flick through this book, remember that these are all *real* questions from *real* computer users. Wherever you'd place yourself on the 'Novice-to-Expert' scale, I'm certain you'll find the answers here to plenty of questions you've wanted to ask yourself!

How to use this book

Like any book, you can obviously read this one from cover to cover if you choose to. (If you do, I'm sure you'll have plenty of *"Gosh, I didn't know that!"* moments.) However, that's not really the intention of the book.

Every question and answer in this book is completely self-contained: you can dip in and out, reading items that look interesting and skipping any that aren't relevant to your specific problem, without needing to read anything that's gone before. More importantly, you can use it as a quick-reference whenever you need an answer to a question of your own; just flip to the appropriate chapter.

Icons and Conventions

Throughout the book I've used a few special features and conventions to make it easier to find your way around and identify important details. In particular, whenever there's a certain procedure to be followed, you'll find it clearly laid out in step-by-step format, with plenty of screenshots, ensuring you can't go wrong.

You'll also find some icons and text in boxes containing other useful information:

An incidental tip relating to the topic you're reading about, a better or quicker way of working, or simply a different way of doing something that you may prefer.

Important extra information about the topic, pointing out anything unusual or unexpected that may crop up along the way, and helping you avoid unforeseen pitfalls.

Quick Tricks to Boost Your Speed

"Everything seems to take me so much time. Are there things I can do to speed things up a bit?"

■ Can I Make Vista Run Faster?

I use Windows Vista, which has become slower and slower. However I'm loath to get rid of this fairly-new operating system and replace it with Windows 7 just yet – is there any way I can speed-up Vista?

You could try Thoosje Vista Tweaker. It's a tool that can make Vista run more quickly, and best of all, it's free. You can download a copy of Thoosje Vista Tweaker using this link: http://www.thoosje.com/Windows-Vista-Tweaker.html. Once you've downloaded and installed the software, restart your PC and then run the application. There are four areas where you can tweak and manage certain Windows behaviours:

• System
• Windows User Interface
• Internet Explorer
• Performance

Not all of them will save you massive amounts of processor time or RAM, but each disabled service will translate to less strain on your processor. Click on each of the icons and you will be presented with a range of features to enable or disable. Once you've selected which components you'd like to disable simply click on **Apply Tweaks**. You should backup your PC before beginning the process just to be on the safe side. Use your own backup utility tool or the one included with Thoosje Vista Tweaker.

■ Windows 7: How Can I Make Accessing My Applications Quicker?

I seem to waste away many minutes of my day trawling through various files and folders to find a program I want to use, so I wondered if you knew of a quicker way to do this? I'm sure it would save me hours and hours over time!

The Windows Start menu is a great way of streamlining the way you get to your most frequently used applications. However, not all the applications are stored there, meaning you indeed have to navigate through the folder structure to find the one you want. Happily you can permanently pin an application, or indeed any file or folder, to the Start menu quite simply. If you'd like to put an application on the Start menu, do the following:

1. Go to **Start > All Programs**.
2. Right-click on the application of your choice and select **Pin to Start menu**.

To un-pin something from the Start menu, do the following:

1. Go to **Start** and right-click on the item you wish to remove.
2. Select **Unpin** from Start menu.

The Start menu is good but it can lack clarity if you have lots of programs in it, not to mention the branches and sub-menus. It's often better to create shortcuts to your frequently-used programs directly on the desktop. This way all you have to do is double-click to open the program. To create an application shortcut, proceed as follows:

1. Go to **Start > All Programs**.
2. Find an application you want to create a shortcut for.
3. Using the right mouse button, drag the icon to a blank space on your desktop.
4. Release the mouse button, and on the little menu that appears, choose **Copy Here**.

■ How Can I Make My Mouse Pointer Move Faster?

I've just bought a new PC and its mouse seems to be very sluggish. If I need to move the pointer from one side of the screen to the other, I have to move the mouse so far on my desk that I run out of space and I have to pick it up and put it down somewhere else. Can anything be done?

The good news is that Windows does make it possible to change the speed at which the pointer moves around the screen. On a new PC you'll often want to adjust this, because Windows initially has the pointer set to move rather slowly. On modern, large screens, that sluggishness becomes even more noticeable because the pointer has further to move than it did on the smaller screens of old. As a result, even if you just replace your monitor you might feel as though your mouse is suddenly struggling to crawl around!

To adjust the speed of the mouse pointer, just follow these steps:

1. Open the Start menu and click **Control Panel**.

2. In the Control Panel window that opens, follow the appropriate step for your version of Windows:
   - **Windows 7:** click the green words **Hardware and Sound**, then click the blue word **Mouse** near the top of the window.
   - **Windows Vista:** in the 'Hardware and Sound' section, click the blue word **Mouse**.
   - **Windows XP:** click **Printers and Other Hardware**, then click **Mouse**.

3. In the Mouse Properties dialog that appears, select the **Pointer Options** tab.

4. The options we need are in the section at the top, headed 'Motion'. First, make sure the checkbox labelled **Enhance pointer precision** is ticked. That makes the pointer a little easier to control when you're moving the mouse slowly and trying to line it up over something small.

5. Next, use the slider to adjust the speed of the pointer, dragging it a little further to the right to make the pointer move around your screen more quickly.

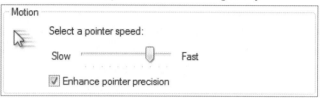

Drag the slider to adjust the speed of the mouse pointer

6. Click the **Apply** button at the bottom of this dialog to put the new settings into effect.

7. Now try moving the mouse pointer around your screen and see what you think of the change. If you feel you've increased the speed too much – or not enough – adjust the slider again and click **Apply** once more to try it out.

8. When you're happy with the new speed, click **OK**.

If you increase the pointer speed by very much, it can feel as though you've overdone it: you'll tend to keep whizzing past the things you're trying to land on with the mouse. You could persevere until you get used to it (as you probably will in a day or two), but you might find it easier to increase the speed by just a small amount now, then follow these steps again in a couple of days to increase it a little more.

■ Speed-up Your PC by Turning Off Visual Effects

I recently bought a new laptop which came with Windows Vista Home Premium. I was expecting it to be a good deal faster than my old computer, but it seems quite a lot slower! Can I do anything to speed it up?

Microsoft has done all it can to make recent versions of Windows as attractive as possible. There are all sorts of 'visual effects' going on that are designed to brighten up our computing experience. For example, menus slide or fade into view rather than just appearing, buttons in Windows 7/Vista flash soothingly when you move the mouse over them, and shadows appear around the edges of windows and the mouse pointer.

The best way to speed-up a Vista computer (and, to a slightly lesser extent, a Windows 7 or XP computer) is to turn off these visual effects. This doesn't change the way you use all the familiar items on your screen, but it does make them look rather different: it will make these recent Windows versions look a lot like the old Windows 2000 or Windows Me.

To choose which visual effects to keep and which to switch off, follow these steps:

1. Right-click the **Computer** or **My Computer** icon on your Start menu or desktop and choose **Properties**.
2. In Windows 7 or Vista, click **Advanced system settings** at the left of the window that opens. In Windows XP, select the **Advanced** tab.
3. In the **Performance** section at the top of the dialog, click the **Settings** button.
4. Now you'll see the dialog pictured in the following

screenshot, containing four option buttons at the top, followed by a list of items with checkboxes beside them. The four options work like this:

- **Let Windows choose what's best for my computer** switches on different effects on different PCs (but generally switches most options on).

- **Adjust for best appearance** switches all the effects on.

- **Adjust for best performance** switches all the effects off.

- **Custom** lets you choose which effects to use by ticking or unticking the items listed below.

5. The best option to choose really depends on how much you want to speed-up your PC, balanced against how much you're going to miss some of these effects. Here's a suggestion: try turning off all the effects by choosing **Adjust for best performance** and then clicking **Apply**. The result will look very different (although not unattractive), but it will give the greatest increase in your PC's speed.

6. You might choose to click **OK** at this point, and try living with this new-look Windows for a while to see how you like it. However, perhaps you miss some of those effects? If so, you can use the checkboxes beside the options in the list to tick the options you'd like to switch back on, clicking **Apply** to put them back into action. The options you'd quite likely want to tick are:

   Show window contents while dragging

   Smooth edges of screen fonts

   Use visual styles on windows and buttons

   Plus these two in Windows 7/Vista:

   Enable desktop composition

   Enable transparent glass

7. If you do decide that Windows was better as it was, and you want all your effects back again, select **Let Windows choose what's best for my computer** and click **OK**.

■ Can I Turn Off My PC When I've Finished Using It?

When I've finished watching TV, all I have to do is press its On/Off switch to turn it off. But when I've finished using my PC I have to go through a complicated 'Shutdown' rigmarole. Is that really necessary? Can't I just switch off my PC in the same way?

There's no escaping the fact that Windows has to be shut down in the correct way before your PC can be switched off. If you simply cut the power to the PC (by unplugging it from the mains, for example) Windows doesn't get the chance to do all the vital tidying up it has to do at the end of your session. If you make a habit of that, sooner or later you'll turn on the PC one day and Windows won't be able to start.

Fortunately, though, there is a way you can press the on/off switch and have Windows shut itself down in an orderly way before turning off your PC. To be able to do that, you'll need to change a setting in Windows. Just follow the appropriate steps for your version of Windows below:

Windows 7/Vista:

1. Open the Start menu and click **Control Panel**.
2. In the Control Panel window that opens, click **System and Security** in Windows 7, or **System and Maintenance** in Windows Vista.
3. Next, click the green word **Power Options** and then, at the left of the window, click **Choose what the power buttons do**.
4. In the next window, open the drop-down list beside the words **When I press the power button** and choose **Shut down**.
5. Click the **Save changes** button at the bottom of the window and then close the window.

Power and sleep button settings

When I press the power button: Shut down

Windows XP:

1. Open the Start menu and click **Control Panel**.
2. In the Control Panel window that opens, click **Performance and Maintenance**, then click **Power Options**.
3. In the dialog that appears, select the **Advanced** tab.

4. In the 'Power buttons' section of this window you can decide what your PC should do when you press its on/off switch. Open the drop-down list beside the words **When I press the power button on my computer** and choose **Shut down**.

5. Click **OK** in this dialog, and then close the Control Panel window.

When I press the power button on my computer:

| Shut down | ⌄ |

From now on, when you've finished work for the day, you can just save any files you were working on, close the programs you were using, and then press your PC's on/off switch. Windows will go straight into its usual shutdown routine and then switch off your PC.

When you use this trick to switch off your PC, be sure to give the power button a fairly quick press (the same way you press the button to switch it on). If you hold the power button for five seconds or so, it cuts the power to the PC, instantly switching it off. Although that might be worth remembering if your PC ever 'locks up' completely and you can't shut it down correctly, it's not something you want to make a habit of! (It's actually very easy to avoid: five seconds is a long time when you're holding a button, so I doubt you'd do it accidentally.)

■ **Windows 7/Vista: Is there a Quicker Way to Search My IE Favorites?**

Over the years I seem to have created quite a collection of Favorites on IE – all of them useful I'm sure! I just can't seem to find my way through them all! Is there a quicker way to navigate through them?

After you've used the Internet for a while, you'll probably find you end up with 1000s of bookmarks or Favorites, which makes finding the one that you want difficult. If you're using Windows 7 or Vista, searching your Favorites is easy – you simply need to create a searchable folder. Once you have created the searchable folder, you can return to it every time you want to find a Favorite. To create the folder, follow these steps:

1. Open Windows Explorer, and navigate to: **C:\Users\<username>**, where <username> is your Windows username.

2. Double-click on **Favorites**.

3. In the search field, type **date:>1/1/2000** to find all Favorites from the last 10 years. Click on the **Save Search** button to save your search.

4. Enter the name **Search Favorites** for the search. The search will be saved to: **C:\Users\<username>\Searches**.

With the searchable folder in place, you can easily search your Favorites as follows:

1. In Windows Explorer, navigate to: **C:\Users\<username>\Searches\Search Favorites**.

2. In the search field, enter a keyword (or just a few letters) from the name or web address of the bookmark you are looking for.

3. The results of your search will be shown in the main window, and you can load the relevant web page by double-clicking on any of the returned results.

To make this quicker still, you could create a shortcut to this Search Favorites item on your desktop for instant access.

■ Is There a Quick Way to Reach My Contacts Folder?

If I open the Start menu, I can get to my Documents and Pictures folders with one click, but not my Contacts folder which I use frequently. Is there a faster way to reach this one?

There are two reasonably quick ways to open your Contacts folder in Windows 7 or Vista:

- Open the Start menu and click your name at the top of the right-hand panel. In the window that appears, double-click the **Contacts** folder.
- Open the Start menu and type the word **contacts** into the Search box at the bottom and then press **Enter**.

An alternative is to create a shortcut to that folder on your desktop. Open the Start menu and click your name, and you'll see the Contacts folder (among others) in the window that opens. Now, using the right mouse button (not the left button!), drag the Contacts folder out of the window and drop it in a blank space on your desktop. On the menu that appears, pictured in the screenshot below, choose **Create shortcuts here**. This will give you a new item named 'Contacts – Shortcut' (although you can rename this to anything you prefer) and you can move it to anywhere you like on your desktop. To open your Contacts folder, just double-click this item.

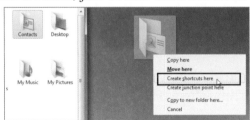

Use the right mouse button to drag your Contacts folder to the desktop and create a shortcut to it

■ Put Your Printer on the Desktop for Quick Access

I'd started printing a long document recently, and realised that I needed to cancel it because there was something I needed to edit first. I was about to click the printer icon that appears beside the clock when it vanished. Why did this happen when the document had barely started printing?

When you start to print something, a little printer icon does indeed appear near the clock on the taskbar, but this doesn't actually indicate that your printer is printing; it just indicates that Windows is sending data to your printer. Even for a large document, Windows may finish doing this quite quickly – long before your printer has finished printing, and perhaps before it's even started – causing that little icon to vanish again.

That's a shame, because while that icon is visible, it gives you a quick way to get at your printer's options: you can click the icon to see which document is printing (and which others are waiting to be printed after it), and cancel printing or pause it temporarily. However, if this is something you ever need to do, or think you may need to do, you can put an icon for your printer permanently on your desktop. Here's how to create that icon:

- **Windows 7/Vista:** open the Start menu and type the word **printers** into the search box at the bottom, then click **Devices and Printers** in Windows 7 or **Printers** in Vista.
- **Windows XP:** open the Start menu and click **Printers and Faxes**.

In the window that appears you'll see several icons (in fact, quite a few in Windows 7), one of which will be the icon for your printer. Simply drag that icon out of this window and drop it on to a blank space on your desktop. (After doing this you can move that new icon to wherever you'd like to place it on your desktop.) You can now close the window you just opened.

From now on, you can get at your printer's options at any time simply by double-clicking this icon. You can pause printing by choosing **Printer > Pause Printing**, continue afterwards by choosing **Printer > Resume Printing**, or cancel printing of the current document by choosing **Document > Cancel**. Best of all, you can do this if even that little printer icon beside the clock has disappeared, essentially meaning that you can ignore that little icon completely.

Chapter 2

Make Your PC A Fortress: Internet and Security

"Help! I'm so worried about security, what can I do to put my mind at rest?"

■ How Can I Keep My Software Up-to-date?

I know it's important to keep my software up-to-date for security reasons, but I find it hard to keep track of which software has an available update. Is there an easier way of keeping track of the software on my PC which needs updating?

Software gets updated all the time and it can be difficult to keep track of everything. Changes are made to make programs more secure and to add features.

With the free Secunia Personal Software Inspector you can always keep your programs updated. The software keeps an overview of the new security updates or program versions without you having to open it. The tool recognises all types of programs and can automatically update them. The update manager searches your computer for installed programs and checks Secunia's online database to see whether newer versions are already available. You can download the program here: http://secunia.com/PSISetup.exe.

When you launch it, the tool searches the hard disk for program files and finds out their versions. You then receive a report as to the available security updates as well as programs that are outdated. You can choose to update each program individually rather than all together. It's best to set aside some time to perform the scan; updating each application can take some time as updates can be very large in size.

■ Why do I Still Have Malware? And How Do I Get Rid of It?

I'm always careful when surfing the web, and try not to click links if I don't know where they go, and never download suspicious-looking software. So why is it

*that my PC ends up with so much malicious software
– and how can I get rid of it?*

It's incredibly easy to end up with malware on your PC.
Even if you are extra careful there is always a chance you
could be infected. To keep your PC safe you should run
comprehensive anti-virus and other security software.
Malwarebytes' Anti-Malware is a free tool that can search
your PC to identify and remove any malware from your
computer. If you believe your PC has been infected, or if
you just want to make sure it's not, get a free copy of the
software. You can download a copy by using this link:
http://www.malwarebytes.org. Once you have
downloaded and installed the software, Malwarebytes'
Anti-Malware will update to the latest database, so ensure
that you are connected to the Internet.

1. Launch Malwarebytes' Anti-Malware.
2. Select the **Perform a quick scan** option.
3. Click on **Scan**.

To make doubly sure that your PC isn't infected you can
perform a full scan as well, but obviously this will take
more time. The length of time the scan takes will depend
upon the size of your hard disk and speed of your PC.

■ **How Can I Get Rid of the Error Message
'Windows Script Host is disabled on
this machine'?**

*Every time I boot my PC and after the Windows
logon screen I get an error message in a window
with the message 'Windows Script Host is disabled
on this machine'. It also happens when I launch
certain applications. How do I get rid of this?*

In order to correct this error, proceed as follows:

1. Switch on the PC and press the **F8** key repeatedly (about twice per second) as the PC is starting. With the arrow keys, select the entry **Safe Mode** and then press the **Enter** key once in Windows 7/Vista or twice in Windows XP.

2. Go to **Start** and type **regedit** in the search box and press **Enter**. (In Windows XP, go to **Start** > **Run**, type **regedit** in the Open box and press **Enter**.)

3. Swap to the key: **HKEY_LOCAL_MACHINE\SOFTWARE\Micro soft\WindowsScript Host\Settings** and right-click on it in the right-hand window.

4. Double-click on **Enabled** in the right-hand window and set the value data to **1**. If the error happens again after you restart, then simply delete the **Enabled** value by right-clicking on it and selecting **Delete** from the dropdown menu.

■ What is a 'Strong' Password (and What is a 'Weak' One)?

When I was signing up for membership on a website I was asked to choose a password. As I typed the password, a little meter alongside was rating my password on a scale between 'weak' and 'strong'. It seemed to think my choice of password was rather weak, but it didn't stop me signing up to the site. I did wonder why this was done, though, and how something like a password could be rated at all. Can you explain?

This password-rating feature is usually just for your benefit. It's fairly rare on websites, but there are some security-related programs that use a similar feature. The point of it is just to let you know whether you've made a good or bad choice of password (and perhaps have a rethink on your choice) – you won't usually be forced to choose something different because your password wasn't regarded as good enough.

So, what is a good (or 'strong') password? Well, the whole reason for a password is to prove your identity. Since no-one but you should know your password, no-one but you should be able to access the information it protects. A strong password is one that no-one should be able to guess.

Rather than rating your password, most sites just insist upon it being a certain length, such as six characters or more. The logic of that is easy: the longer a password, the more difficult it should be to guess.

However, it's not brilliant logic in this day and age. By those terms, the word 'superstitious' should be an excellent password because it's a massive 13 letters long (somewhat ironically). Unfortunately, it's weak. If someone badly wants to crack their way in, they can use a 'dictionary attack': a computer program simply tries every word in the dictionary until it finds the right one. There are a lot of words in a dictionary, of course, but computers are fast and, unlike people, have few pressing engagements, so they can be left to get on with it.

To make a password stronger, then, avoid using words that are in the dictionary, or use an unusual mixture of capital and small letters. Better still, and sure to gain a high rating, is a password that combines capital and small letters with numbers. For humans and computers alike, this would take years to guess.

By definition, unfortunately, a strong password is going to be a long, strange one that's difficult to remember.

You have to weigh up the sensitivity of the information being protected and decide whether it warrants the effort of remembering a really strong password or not. Online banking accounts certainly do, for example, but membership of a chat website probably doesn't.

■ Windows 7/Vista: Safely Edit the Hosts File After a Virus Attack

I've just managed to get my system working again after a virus attack, but I have one problem remaining: I still can't reach certain websites. Whether I choose an item from my Favorites list or type the address myself, I end up at a completely different site from the one I wanted. What could be causing this?

When a virus attacks your system, it will often modify the hosts file to add fake IP addresses for popular websites, in order to create so-called Phishing attacks. This means that when you visit the site for your online bank, for example, you are redirected to a fake website, designed to look like the real website you are trying to access, which steals password and username details. Although your anti-virus software can remove the infection from your system, it will probably not clear the hosts file (located in C:\Windows\System32\drivers \etc\hosts), so after removing an infection from your system you should also check the hosts file for website names and remove any you find.

However, in Windows 7 and Vista you may see an error telling you that access to the hosts file was denied, or telling you to check that the path and filename are correct. If this happens, then you can edit the file by following these steps:

1. Click **Start** > **All Programs** > **Accessories**, right-click **Notepad**, and then click **Run as administrator.**

2. If you are prompted for an Administrator password or for a confirmation, type the password, or click **Allow** or **Yes**.

3. Choose **File** > **Open**.

4. Change the file filter from **Text Documents (*.txt)** to **All Files**.

5. Browse to **C:\Windows\System32\drivers\etc**, select the **Hosts** file and click **Open**.

6. Edit the file as necessary to remove any lines containing the addresses of websites.

7. Click **File** > **Save** to save your changes.

■ Is Adobe Flash Player Safe to Install?

On various websites, I keep getting a security message asking if I wish to install Adobe Flash Player. I do not know what this is, or whether it would be any use to me if I did install it. Can you advise?

As a very important rule of thumb, if you visit a website and are asked whether you wish to install something, you should say No. This is the most common method by which malicious software is installed on your computer, and the dangers of malicious software far outweigh the benefits of any legitimate software, so it's never worth taking risks.

Having said that, not all software installed in this way is malicious or dangerous, and the program named Adobe Flash Player is safe. This program is published by a company named Adobe Systems Incorporated. If you're asked whether you want to install this program, and the name of its publisher is correct, then it's safe to go ahead. The installation is quick and entirely automatic.

This is a popular piece of software that shows animations, music players and videos on websites, and it's used by a growing number of sites. If you haven't installed it, you'll be prompted to do so every time you visit one of the sites that uses it. If you're in the wise habit of saying 'No' to these prompts, it's certainly fine to refuse this program too, but in this particular case the program does allow some useful or enjoyable features of websites to be displayed.

■ Why Does Internet Explorer Ask About 'Content that was Delivered Securely'?

Each time I log into my online banking page, Internet Explorer asks me whether I want to see only content that was delivered securely. Should I be choosing 'Yes' or 'No' to this?

Any web page that deals with your private information should be 'secure'. In other words, the information the website sends to display in your browser, and the information you send back to the website (by filling in a form, for instance) should be encrypted, ensuring that if anyone intercepts it, they won't be able to decipher it or use it.

To get a bit technical for a moment, ordinary non-secure web pages use a system called HTTP to transfer information between you and the website: at one of these pages, if you look at the address bar at the top of your browser, you'll see that its address begins with 'http://'. Secure web pages use a system named 'HTTPS' (the added 'S' stands for 'Secure'), and at these pages you'll see that the address begins with 'https://'.

At a secure page, it's not just the web page itself that should be sent securely, but any other files used by that web page. Most pages contain pictures, for example, and there may well be other types of file that the page has to load from the website to make it work correctly. Sometimes, however, mistakes by the web page's designer result in the page itself being delivered securely, but one or more of its extra files being delivered via the ordinary, non-secure system.

In the vast majority of cases, this won't matter at all, but Internet Explorer feels that it's best to warn you, just in case, and asks what you want to do about it.

In general, the best choice is to display only the secure items and skip the non-secure items. Unfortunately, Internet Explorer asks its question in two different ways, depending on which version you're using:

Internet Explorer 8:

In IE8 you'll see the dialog pictured in the next screenshot, which asks whether you want to view only the secure items. In this case, choose **Yes**.

Internet Explorer 7 and earlier:

In earlier versions of Internet Explorer, the question asked is whether you want to view the non-secure items. In this case, the answer should be **No**.

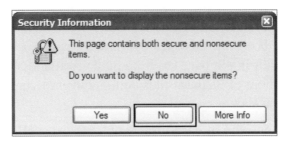

Chapter 3

Organise and Manage Your Photos Easily

"I'm getting in such a mess with all my digital photos. How am I supposed to keep track of them all?"

■ How Can I Save a Photo Attachment to the 'My Pictures' Folder?

For the first time, a photo has been sent to me as an email attachment which I would like to keep. I want to save it in the 'My Pictures' folder, but I have no idea how to do it. Can you explain?

Assuming you're using either Windows Mail (in Windows Vista) or Outlook Express (in Windows XP), here are the steps you need:

1. Click the paperclip button at the top-right of the message, and then click **Save Attachments** on the menu that appears.

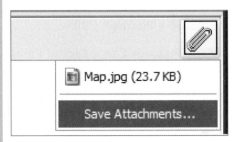

Click the paperclip button

2. Now you'll see the dialog pictured in the next screenshot. In this dialog, click the **Browse** button.

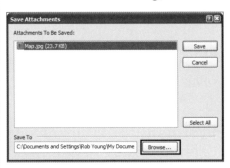

*Click **Browse** to choose where to save the picture*

3. Next you'll see another dialog titled 'Browse for

Folder' which lets you choose which folder to save the attachment into. In Vista, you may see your 'Pictures' folder straight away: if so, just click it once to select it, then click **OK** and jump to step 5 below. If you don't see the folder, continue to step 4.

4. Scroll to the top of the list of folders and then do the following:

   • In Windows Vista, click the little arrow beside the folder that's named after you, which reveals the folders inside it. One of these will be your 'Pictures' folder (although you may have to scroll downward a little way to see it). Click that folder, then click **OK**.

   • In Windows XP, click the + sign beside the 'My Documents' folder to see the folders inside it. One of these will be your 'My Pictures' folder. Click that folder, then click **OK**.

Select your 'My Pictures' (or 'Pictures') folder

5. Now you'll be back at the Save Attachments dialog pictured in step 2. All that remains to do is to click the **Save** button at the top-right of that dialog, and

the attachment will be saved into your Pictures (or My Pictures) folder.

■ How Can I Print Photos from a Web Page?

My daughter has put photos of her family holiday in an online photo album. Although I can see the pictures, I haven't been able to print them successfully. When I try, I either get a collection of small pictures and text or just one small picture. What am I doing wrong?

An online photo album is essentially a web page (or several pages) containing pictures, so you'll be viewing it in your web browser, such as Internet Explorer. The person who created the album will send you a link to the web page, and perhaps a password you'll have to enter when you arrive (if they wanted to keep the album private rather than allowing the whole world to see it).

The album itself will be a collection of small pictures, similar to the following screenshot. If you were to print this page, you'd get exactly what you see on the screen: those small versions of the pictures laid out in the same way, along with any other text on the web page.

A little experimentation might lead you to right-click one of these small pictures. The menu that appears will contain a 'Print Picture' option, but unfortunately this isn't what you want either: it will print the small version of the picture.

When you move the mouse over one of the small pictures, however, you'll see that it turns into a hand shape, indicating that the picture links to something. Click the picture and you'll be whisked to another page showing a full-size version of the picture. It's this version of the picture that you want to print.

If you now right-click this picture, you'll see the menu pictured below:

Choose the Print (or better, Save) Picture option

There are two ways to proceed from here, but the second is generally the one to choose:

- **Print Picture:** you can choose this option to print the picture directly from Internet Explorer. You'll see a Print dialog, and by clicking the **Preferences** you can set up printer options such as paper size and quality before printing.

- **Save Picture As:** you can choose this option to save the full-size picture to your computer. This is the better option to choose if there's a particular program on your PC that you use to print photos (such as the Windows Photo Gallery program in Windows Vista). Not only will you be able to print the photo using a familiar program, but you'll also be able to keep the picture (if you want to) as part of your collection. After you click **Save Picture As** you'll see an ordinary Save As dialog letting you choose where to save the picture and what to name it.

Whichever option you pick, after saving or printing the picture click your browser's **Back** button to return to the album of small pictures and click another to view at full size in the same way.

■ Can I Enlarge a Picture?

I've often seen explanations of how to reduce the size of photos, but I have the opposite question. A relative has sent me a family photo by email, and it's very small and rather indistinct. Is it possible to enlarge it?

In strictly technical terms, yes it is. However, you may not be too thrilled with the result, so it would be best to ask whether anyone has the original, full-size photo before you resort to enlarging this small one!

When a photo is reduced in size, you start with more information than you need. If you halve the size of a photo, for instance, three out of every four pixels (dots) is removed, but a program can use the colours of those three pixels to work out the best colour for the single pixel that remains, so that the human eye shouldn't notice anything has gone missing.

If you double the size of a picture, three pixels have to

be added for each pixel in the original, but there's nothing to tell a program what colour those added pixels should be. It has to do a little guesswork based on the colours surrounding the pixel it's adding to. The resulting picture will be twice the size of the original, but it won't – and can't – be any more detailed, and will be starting to look a little blurred. The more you enlarge it, the more blurred it will look.

If you'd like to try enlarging a picture, the Paint program included with Windows is as good as anything to do the job:

1. Go to **Start** > **All Programs** > **Accessories** > **Paint**.

2. In the Paint window, do the following:

   • In Windows 7, click the blue tab at the far left of the Ribbon and choose **Open**.

   • In Windows Vista/XP, choose **File** > **Open**.

3. In the Open dialog, find and select the picture you want to edit and click the **Open** button.

4. When the picture appears in the Paint window, you're ready to resize it. Start by following the appropriate step below:

   • In Windows 7, make sure the **Home** tab is selected on the Ribbon and click the **Resize** button in the 'Image' section.

- In Windows Vista, choose **Image > Resize/Skew**.

- In Windows XP, choose **Image > Stretch/Skew**.

5. Now you'll see a dialog similar to the one pictured below. Type the figure **200** into the two boxes at the top (i.e. 200%, or double the current size) and click **OK**.

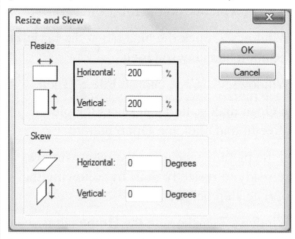

Be sure to type the same figure into both boxes!

6. Paint will enlarge the picture to double its current size. You can press **Ctrl+S** if you're happy to replace the original, smaller image with this new one. If you'd prefer to save this with a new name, keeping the small version as well, click the blue tab on the Ribbon in Windows 7 and choose **Save As**, or choose **File > Save As** in Windows Vista/XP, and type a different name for this picture.

■ How Many Pictures Can a Digital Camera Store on a Memory Card?

I need to buy a memory card for my new digital camera, and I don't know what to choose. It seems that more expensive memory cards can hold more pictures, but they don't say how many. Can you advise me?

Memory cards are the small disk-like devices you insert into a digital camera to store the pictures you take. (By 'disk-like' I don't mean that they look like disks – they have a rectangular plastic case with nothing circular inside it – but they behave just like your hard disk or a floppy disk).

The most important aspect of a memory card is its capacity – how much space it has for storing pictures. In general, cheap memory cards have a low-capacity, and the capacity increases the more you spend. At the low end you'll find memory cards with capacities of 128 MB costing just a few pounds; at the higher end there are cards offering a huge 4 GB at a much higher price.

When you buy a digital camera, it usually comes with a memory card, but one with an absolutely tiny capacity – sometimes a paltry 16 MB – which may hold no more than half-a-dozen photos. You'll almost always have to buy a higher-capacity card for any serious use.

The other important consideration is the size of the pictures your camera takes. This is a figure measured in 'megapixels' which will probably be shown on the camera itself, and will certainly be mentioned in its manual. To determine how many pictures will fit on to a memory card of a particular capacity, you need to know how much space each picture will occupy.

When you know the megapixel figure of your camera, the table below will tell you how many pictures will fit on to different capacities of memory card. (This table assumes that you'll be taking pictures using your camera's best quality settings. If you reduce the quality settings on your camera, you'll fit more pictures on to the card.)

Pictures per card	128 MB	256 MB	512 MB	1 GB	2 GB	4 GB
3 megapixel camera	100	200	400	800	1600	3200
4 megapixel camera	80	160	320	640	1280	2560
5 megapixel camera	60	120	240	480	960	1920
6 megapixel camera	50	100	200	400	800	1600
7 megapixel camera	40	80	160	320	640	1280
8 megapixel camera	35	70	140	280	560	1120

Before you buy a memory card, make sure that your digital camera is able to use a card with your chosen capacity. In particular, some cameras won't work with very-high-capacity cards. Your camera's manual will tell you if there are any limits on the capacity of card you can use.

Remember that memory cards are intended to be reused: you're not trying to gather a lifetime of photography on this card so you probably don't need a card with a huge capacity. As long as the card can hold all the pictures you'll take on one outing, you can then copy them to your PC, empty the card, and use it again next time.

Another point to remember is that you don't have to limit yourself to just one memory card. If you have two or three smaller-capacity cards, just take them all with you when you go out. When one is full, you pop it out of the camera, store it safely in its case and insert another to carry on snapping.

■ Create a Contact Sheet of Pictures in Windows Photo Gallery

I use Windows Photo Gallery in Windows Vista to print my photos. I'm told there's a way to print a contact sheet containing several photos, but I can't seem to find it. Can you explain how it's done?

A contact sheet is a sort of index of your photos: it's a single sheet which contains small versions of up to 35 different photos. You certainly can print contact sheets in Windows Photo Gallery, but only if you make the right choices at every step along the way. Here's how to do it:

1. After starting Windows Photo Gallery, select the folder containing the photos you want to print.

2. Next, select all the photos you want to include on your contact sheet. You can press **Ctrl+A** to select all the photos in the folder, or choose individual photos by holding down the **Ctrl** key and clicking each required photo in turn.

3. When you've selected the photos you want, click the **Print** button on the black toolbar and select **Print**.

4. Now you'll see the 'Print Pictures' window. The first thing to do here is to open the drop-down list labelled **Paper size** and choose a larger-than-normal paper size, because contact sheets can only be printed on to large sheets of paper. The best choice is usually **A4** but you could also choose **8" x 10"** if you have 8-by-10-inch photo paper.

5. Next, select the type of paper you'll be printing on to from the **Paper type** list, and choose the required printing quality from the **Quality** list.

6. Now, if you look at the right panel of the window, you'll see a variety of layouts and, towards the

bottom, you'll see the two we're interested in: **Wallet** and **Contact sheet**. The **Wallet** option prints 9 photos per page, making each a fairly reasonable size; the **Contact sheet** option fits 35 pictures on a page (obviously making them much smaller!) and also includes the names of the photos. Click whichever of these layouts you'd like to use, and the preview in the main section of the window will update you and show you how the printed result should look. Below the preview itself you'll see a note of how many pages are needed to print all the photos you selected. If they run to more than one page, you can use the arrow buttons to move back and forth between pages. You can also switch back and forth between **Wallet** and **Contact sheet** comparing the two and deciding which you prefer.

7. When you're happy with your choices, click **Print** to print your contact sheet on paper.

■ Why Do I No Longer See Thumbnails of My Pictures?

Until recently, when I opened my Pictures folder I'd see small versions of all my pictures. Now all I see are ordinary-looking icons and I can't tell which picture is which.

Normally, when you open your **Pictures** or **My Pictures** folder, you'd expect to see thumbnails of all your pictures, as shown on the left in the next screenshot. Rather unhelpfully, though, Windows might just display generic icons instead (shown on the right in the screenshot).

In Windows 7 and Vista, the cause could be that you've installed a picture-editing program which has changed some settings, or perhaps you experimented with the settings yourself. Either way, just follow these steps to put things right:

1. Click the **Organize** button near the top left of the window and select **Folder and search options**.
2. In the Folder Options dialog that appears, select the **View** tab.
3. Remove the tick beside **Always show icons, never thumbnails**.
4. Click **OK**.

In Windows XP, the cause and the solution are both simple. The cause is that XP sometimes just 'forgets' you want to see thumbnails, and the easy fix is to open the **View** menu at the top of the window and click **Thumbnails**.

■ Can I Remove Picasa Without Losing My Photos?

I installed Picasa, but I don't really like it and I'm thinking of uninstalling it. However, as it's taken over all my pictures, I'm worried that I'll lose them all along with Picasa. Should I copy them all somewhere before removing Picasa?

This is a common concern with programs like Picasa, but a completely mistaken one. Picasa isn't storing your photos in any way: like all your other files, your photos are stored safely on your hard disk. All Picasa does is to find out which folder (or folders) they're stored in and then display them as a kind of catalogue or index to give you easy access to them all from one friendly program.

Although it's certainly sensible to keep copies of your photos (and all your other personal documents) on a separate disk for safety, you can uninstall programs like Picasa without any risk at all to the pictures and other personal files on your PC. Indeed, any program that did delete any of your personal files when you uninstalled it would be regarded as an extremely malicious program that we (and many others) would go to great lengths to warn you about!

Chapter 4

Get to Know Your Hardware – and Start Using it YOUR Way

"Hardware and how to improve it is mentioned everywhere, but I don't understand what it means. Help!"

■ What's the Difference Between a 'Disk' and a 'Drive'?

The words 'disk' and 'drive' appear frequently in computing articles and magazines, but I'm never sure of the difference between them. Can you explain?

The terms do tend to be used interchangeably, particularly in terms like 'hard disk' and 'hard drive', but the two words do technically relate to different things.

A 'disk' is a device on which computer files are stored, and a 'drive' is a mechanical device that reads what's on the disk or writes more files on to it. A good example is a CD: the disk itself holds computer files, but in order to get them there or to use them, you have to put that disk in a CD drive. Likewise, a floppy disk holds files, but you have to insert the disk in a floppy disk drive (sometimes shortened to 'floppy drive') to read or add files.

The terms get a little muddled for hard disks, because the disk itself is permanently sealed inside the drive – you only see the drive if you open up your computer, and you should never try to open the drive itself to see its disk! Nevertheless, there is a disk in there (in fact, there are several) containing your files, and the drive is the casing that encloses it and does the mechanical job of spinning the disk and reading or writing data. In a nutshell, then, a drive is a thing you need to read the data stored on a disk.

■ Can I Use a Mouse with My Notebook PC?

I have a notebook computer, and instead of a mouse it has a square pad that I drag my finger over to move the pointer on the screen. I find this difficult to use, so I wondered if it's possible to use a normal mouse instead?

Yes, it certainly is. That square pad is called a 'trackpad', and it isn't everyone's cup of tea, but it has the benefit that it's built into the notebook PC. As a notebook PC is supposed to be portable, most people don't want to carry around extra bits and pieces that have to be plugged into it. However, as more and more of us keep our notebook PCs on our desks and rarely carry them around, it's no problem to plug in an ordinary mouse.

Indeed, it really is as simple as that. Assuming your PC has a USB socket (as all notebooks made in the last 10 years do), you can simply visit a computer store, buy a USB mouse and plug it into a USB socket. The computer will recognise it and get it working automatically within a few seconds, and you're away.

One extra thing you might want to do is to disable the trackpad to avoid brushing it accidentally. The way you do this can vary from one trackpad to another, but in the majority of cases you go to **Start** > **Control Panel** and choose the **Mouse** item, and one of the tabs in the window that appears will relate to your trackpad. Select that tab, and you should find an option to either disable the trackpad completely, or to disable it whenever a normal mouse is plugged in.

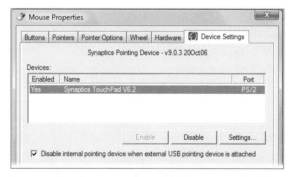

Most trackpads can be disabled if you prefer to use a mouse

■ How Much Space is Left on My Hard Disk?

How can I find out how much space I have left on my hard disk?

The steps to find this information are very straightforward – in fact, you can use the same steps to find out the total size and available space of any type of disk (with a couple of provisos that I'll mention in a moment).

1. Click the **Computer** or **My Computer** item on your Start menu.

2. In the window that opens you'll see icons for each of the drives attached to your computer. Right-click the icon for your hard drive (named C:), or whichever drive you're interested in, and choose **Properties** from the context menu that appears.

*Right-click a drive icon and choose **Properties***

Apart from hard disks, which are always available, most other types of drive use removable disks so it's possible for the drive you select to be empty. To find information about a removable disk such as a floppy disk, memory card or CD, make sure you insert the disk into the appropriate drive before right-clicking the drive's icon.

3. As long as the drive you right-clicked was a hard drive (or some other kind of drive with a disk inserted), you'll now see the dialog pictured in the next screenshot, containing a useful collection of information.

The first thing you'll notice is the colourful chart in the middle. This gives you a quick view of how much space is used on the disk (shown in blue) and how much is still available (shown in pink). If you'd like to know in more precise terms, have a look at the numbers shown above the chart. As the screenshot shows, my hard disk's total size is 114 GB (gigabytes), of which I've used 43 GB, so I have about 71 GB still available to store more files.

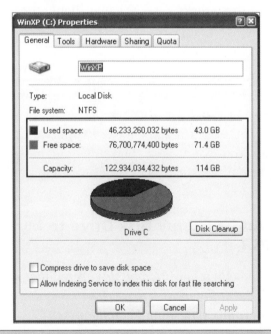

Don't be surprised if the 'Capacity' of the disk is somewhat less than you thought it was. A certain amount of space on any disk has to be set aside to store a sort of 'table of contents' that allows the system to find files on

> the disk, and this chunk of space is ignored. My hard disk is actually 120 GB, but the screenshot shows its size as 114 GB; the missing 6 GB is what was used to create its table of contents.

Although you can use these steps to find the same information about any disk, bear in mind that for some types of disk the information won't be very helpful. In particular, the figures for CD-ROM and DVD disks will always indicate that there's no free space at all, and the total capacity shown will be the same as the amount of space used. This is because you can't add more files to a CD or DVD, all you can do is to use the files that are there already; therefore, Windows avoids giving the impression that these disks have space available for you to use.

> Along with finding out the total size of a disk, you can use a similar method to find out the size of a folder (including all the files it contains), or the size of an individual file. Just find the file or folder you're interested in, right-click it and choose **Properties** in the same way. You won't see a chart this time, but you will see figures giving the exact size of the item you clicked.

■ Can I Add a Floppy Disk Drive to My New PC?

I've just bought a new PC and discovered that it doesn't have a floppy disk drive. Can I install one, and if so, is this something I can do myself?

Floppy disks are slow and unreliable, and in recent years they've been superseded by newer and better solutions such as CDs, DVDs, flash drives and home networks. As a result, many new PCs come with no floppy disk drive.

That's a shame, because floppy disks are still useful for copying small files from one PC to another, or sharing files with friends. Moreover, if you've got files stored on floppy disks (which, as I hinted, is risky because floppy disks are notoriously unreliable!), you can't get at those files without a floppy disk drive.

You can buy a floppy disk drive to fit into your PC and they cost only a few pounds. However, fitting one involves opening the computer's case, physically installing it, and connecting it to an available power cable and data cable from the bunch of cables inside the case. It's rather fiddly, and you always run the risk of damaging other components in the process as well as perhaps invalidating your PC's warranty.

Here's a far better solution: look for a USB floppy disk drive. You'll find these in many good computer and electronics stores at around £20, so they're not much more expensive than the traditional type of floppy disk drive that has to be fitted inside the computer's case. The great benefit of the USB version is that it's extremely easy to use: just connect the USB cable from the back of the drive to a USB socket on your PC, and within seconds it will be ready-for-use. (Of course, it has the additional flexibility that you can connect it to absolutely any PC.)

A USB floppy disk drive is cheap and easy to use

■ Why Has My Laptop's Wireless Connection Disappeared?

Until this morning, whenever I started my laptop it would automatically connect to my wireless network and give me Internet access. Today, it hasn't done that and it won't even admit that I have a network to connect to! All I see is a red 'x' covering the network icon beside the clock and the words 'Not connected'. When I click that icon to try to connect, not only is my own network missing, I can't even see my neighbours' networks.

There are two good clues here as to what has happened. The first is that you're using a laptop, and the second is that no wireless networks at all are available, not even those of your neighbours.

To connect to a wireless network, a computer needs a device called a 'wireless adapter'. In most laptops made within the last few years, the wireless adapter is built into the PC, whereas for desktop PCs (and older computers in general) you have to buy this adapter as a separate gadget and plug it in.

Those modern laptops also have a feature that seems carefully designed to catch out the unwary: somewhere on your laptop's case you'll find a switch that turns this wireless adapter on and off. The cause of the problem is almost certainly that you've accidentally turned this switch off, with the result that your laptop behaves as if it had no wireless adapter built into it and therefore can't see your wireless network (or any other wireless networks within range of your PC). The obvious solution, then, is to find this switch and turn it back on. Within a few seconds, your laptop should find and connect to your wireless network as it always has done.

Let's return briefly to the fact that you couldn't see your neighbours' wireless networks either – in what way is that a clue? Well, your wireless adapter would normally present a list of all the networks within range, and you're quite likely used to seeing the names of your neighbours' networks in this list along with your own. The fact that these had also disappeared indicates that your wireless adapter was switched off.

If you had been able to see your neighbours' networks, and only your own was missing, it would indicate that your wireless adapter was working but that your own network wasn't available. The likely reason for that is that your router is switched off or has developed a problem: assuming it hasn't given up the ghost entirely, the solution should be to switch the router off for a minute or two and then switch it back on again.

It's also possible for your wireless adapter to give up the ghost too, and that would obviously produce the same result – that your PC was unable to see or connect to any wireless networks. However, it's far more likely that you've accidentally switched it off. If you use a desktop PC rather than a laptop and you have the same problem, try unplugging the wireless adapter for a few seconds and then plugging it back in again.

■ Help! Everything on My Screen Has Stretched!

A computer engineer recently adjusted my screen settings so that I would be able to view large photos. (Previously I only saw a piece at a time and had to scroll to different portions of a picture.) At first I liked the change, but all my text and icons had become much smaller and difficult to see clearly. I tried to change the setting to something halfway between where it was originally and where the engineer set it, but now everything has become stretched – text and icons are now very tall and thin, and look very odd. Why has this happened?

The setting in question is called 'screen resolution', and it relates to the number of dots used to make up the picture on the screen. To explain how it works, let's use the example of an icon (like the ones you see on your desktop). An icon is 32 dots wide and 32 dots high.

If your screen resolution is set to use a small number of dots, every dot on your screen will be quite large. As a result, the icons will look bigger because they will be 32 big dots wide and 32 big dots high.

If your screen resolution is set to use more dots, all the dots on your screen will be smaller. Therefore, icons are 32 smaller dots wide by 32 smaller dots high, so all the icons look smaller.

Of course, this applies to everything else you see on your screen too: pictures, text, buttons, menus, you name it. If you set your screen to use more dots, everything will get a little smaller, and you'll be able to see more on the screen at once.

First I'll show you how to change the resolution, but before you actually follow these steps, be sure to read to the end of this question:

Windows 7:

1. Right-click a blank space on the desktop and click **Personalize**.
2. Click **Display** near the bottom-left of the window, followed by **Adjust resolution** near the top-left.
3. You'll see drop-down list labelled **Resolution**: make

a mental note of its current setting.

4. Open the **Resolution** box and you'll see a slide you can use to adjust the resolution. Drag it upwards to make the dots smaller (a higher resolution) or downwards to make them larger (a lower resolution), then click **Apply** to see the result.

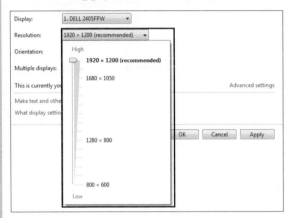

5. If you're happy with the result, click **OK**. If you're not, follow step 4 again, either to try a different setting or to return to the original setting.

Windows Vista/XP:

1. Right-click a blank space on the desktop and choose **Personalize** in Vista or **Properties** in Windows XP.

2. In Windows Vista, click the blue text that says **Display Settings**. In other versions of Windows choose the **Settings** tab.

3. You'll see the words 'Screen resolution' (or just 'Resolution') with a slider below them. Make a mental note of where this slider currently is by noting the numbers shown below it (such as '800 by 600 pixels').

4. Drag this slider to the right to make the dots smaller (a higher resolution) or the left to make them larger (a

lower resolution) then click **Apply** to see the result.

5. If you're happy with the result, click **OK**. If you're not, follow step 4 again, either to try a different setting or to return to the original setting.

Picking a high resolution makes your graphics card work harder, and all graphics cards have a maximum resolution they can cope with. Although the slider can be used to pick a very high resolution, your graphics card won't necessarily be able to handle it. After you change the resolution, Windows should display a dialog asking if you're happy to keep the new setting. If you see this dialog, and your screen looks okay, click **Yes**. If you see the dialog and your screen doesn't look good, click **No** and try again. If your screen goes black and nothing happens, DON'T DO ANYTHING! Just wait about 15 seconds and don't touch the mouse or keyboard. What has happened is that your graphics card can't cope with the new resolution, but after about 15 seconds, Windows will realise you didn't say 'Yes' in the dialog it showed (because you can't see it!) and will automatically put your screen back to how it was before.

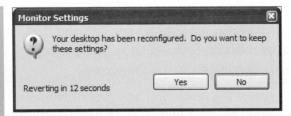

*Windows shows this dialog after changing resolution; click **Yes** if you're happy with the screen display*

Those are the steps, but as the questioner discovered, it's possible to end up with a strange result. Here's the reason: by dragging the slider, you're choosing from a range of preset sizes, but those sizes won't all match the shape of your screen. Some of them are for wide-screen monitors, while others are for the more square shape of monitor.

It all comes down to ratios. The square type of monitor has a ratio of 4:3 so you can use these resolutions:

• 640x480

• 800x600

• 1024x768

• 1152x864

• 1280x1024

• 1600x1200

Widescreen monitors usually have a ratio of 16:9 or 16:10, so any other resolutions you see when you drag the slider will be for widescreen (or small, letterbox-shaped) screens.

If you're using a square 4:3 monitor and you pick one of the widescreen resolutions, your monitor tries to pack an awful lot of dots widthways and comparatively few dots lengthways. Going back to our icon example, the icon is now 32 very-small dots wide and 32 rather-big dots high! In other words, the icon is very thin and stretched very tall. And, of course, the same is true of text, pictures and everything else on the screen.

So, if you change the resolution and everything seems to have stretched to become unusually tall or unusually wide, you've picked a resolution that doesn't suit the shape of your screen. Of course, the solution is to pick a different resolution:

- If you have a squarish (4:3) monitor, choose one of the resolutions I listed above.

- If you have a widescreen monitor, pick a resolution that doesn't appear in the list above. In this case, you may still notice that items on the screen are very slightly stretched in one direction or the other, or appear blurred. If so, you've picked a 16:9 resolution when you have a 16:10 monitor, or vice versa, so try one of the other resolutions (again picking one that doesn't appear in the list above).

■ Make Your Printer Remember Your Settings

I've recently bought a new printer and discovered that it can print in 'draft mode' to save ink. I set it to draft mode and noticed a difference in the print-quality which indicated that it certainly was using less ink, but today it's gone back to normal mode. Why is that, and will I have to select draft mode every time I print something?

When you have a program open and you decide to print your current document, you choose **File > Print** and a Print dialog appears. Here you can click a **Properties** or **Preferences** button to choose settings specific to your printer, such as its print-quality. Most good printers offer a choice of print-quality modes, such as a 'draft' mode that uses less ink (ideal when you're printing something for your own reference), or a choice between black-and-white and colour printing.

*Before printing, click **Preferences** or **Properties** to adjust your printer's settings*

After choosing the printer settings you want to use, you can go ahead and print the document. If you keep the same program open and print another document afterwards, the settings you chose will be used when printing that document too.

However, the settings you've chosen only apply to the program you're using, and only until you close that program. So, if you usually want to print things in draft mode and black-and-white, but your printer normally prints in high-quality colour, you have to keep choosing your preferred print settings before printing.

There is a way to tell your printer which settings you want it to use and make it remember them, though. By doing this, you can tell it to always print in draft mode black-and-white unless you specify something different. Here's how to make your printer remember the settings you prefer:

1. Begin by following the appropriate step below:

   • **Windows 7**: go to **Start > Control Panel**, then click **View devices and printers** in the 'Hardware and Sound' section.

   • **Windows Vista**: go to **Start > Control Panel** and click **Printer** in the 'Hardware and Sound' section.

   • **Windows XP**: go to **Start > Printers and Faxes**.

2. When you arrive you'll see one or more icons in the window (quite a few more in Windows 7, in fact). One of these will be an icon representing your printer: it may have a slightly odd-looking name, but you should recognise it as being similar to the make and/or model of your printer.

3. Right-click your printer's icon and choose **Properties**.

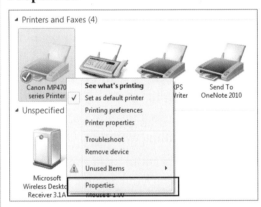

4. Now you'll see exactly the same dialog I mentioned earlier, presenting all your printer's options and settings. The one difference is that having arrived at it via the steps above, any changes you make now

will 'stick'. You can choose the option to print in 'draft' mode, for example, and in future anything you print – from any program – will be printed in 'draft' mode.

Of course, you can follow the same steps again whenever you like if you want to change the default printing settings.

■ Why Does My PC Keep Switching Itself Off?

All of a sudden, my PC has started switching itself off for no apparent reason. It usually happens within about half-an-hour of switching on, and there's no warning and no proper shutdown – it just switches off. What's the problem?

There are two possible causes of this, both hardware-related. It's just possible that the problem is with the computer's electrics – that the power supply unit (PSU) inside its case, which supplies power to all the other internal gadgetry, is on its last legs. However, by far the more likely cause is that the PC is overheating.

Computers have a sort of 'self-protection' mechanism that keeps an eye on the temperature of the vital (and expensive!) processor. When the PC is having to work hard, it's normal for the temperature to rise, but this mechanism has ways of dealing with that. One is to start or speed-up the PC's internal fan (or fans), sucking air through vents in the case and blowing it over the processor to cool it down. The other, if the situation is getting more desperate, is to make the processor work more slowly until the temperature drops again, but that won't necessarily make much difference since other gadgets inside the case are also generating heat.

If the temperature gets seriously high, that protection mechanism cuts off the PC's power to prevent the processor's core from melting. A good way to prove that this is what has happened is to try switching on the PC again straight away: you'll probably find that nothing happens – the temperature is still too high, so this mechanism won't allow the PC to start. After another few minutes, it probably will start, confirming the diagnosis, but it's best to switch it off again (after shutting down Windows in an orderly way) as soon as you can, before it cuts the power again.

Before you take your PC to be fixed, there are a few things you can do yourself. First, check whether the vents in your PC's case are clogged up with dust, hair and lunch: if they are, the fans will struggle to draw in any cool air. A flick with a duster will remove this easily (and it's worth doing this regularly to prevent a build-up).

Inevitably, some of this muck and rubbish will find its way inside the case through the vents, and (thanks to the fans) will end up coating all the components. With the PC switched off and unplugged, remove the PC's side panel and check the state of its innards. If it's looking a bit dusty, try blowing the dust out. Pay particular attention to any fans you see (there may be more than one).

Leaving the computer's side panel off, plug in and switch on the PC and watch to see if the fans spin. However clean they are, it's possible that a fan has simply gone to meet its maker, and that would account for the overheating. If Windows does start, use the usual Shut Down procedure to switch off the PC, then unplug it before putting the side panel of the case back on.

Chapter 5

Software Problems Fixed Instantly

"When I install software, there always seems to be a problem. How can I stop this from happening?"

■ How Do I Backup My Registry?

I frequently read articles which tell me how to make a registry tweak to fix software problems and bugs. But they always tell me to backup my registry before I begin. How do I go about doing this?

As you point out, before you apply any registry tweaks or security fixes to your PC you should always make a backup of your system's registry. To do so, follow the appropriate set of steps below.

To backup the registry in Windows 7 by setting a Manual System Restore Point:

1. Click **Start > Control Panel > System**.
2. Click on the link **System Protection**, then click **Create**.
3. Enter a name for your restore point, then click **OK**.
4. Once the restore point has been created, click **Close > OK**.

To backup the registry in Windows Vista Home Premium/Vista Home Basic by setting a Manual System Restore Point:

1. Click **Start**.
2. Type: **Sys** and then wait for the search results to appear.
3. Under Programs, click **System Restore**.
4. If the User Account Control dialog appears, click **Continue**.
5. Click **open System Protection**.
6. Under **Available Disks**, tick one or more drives. Remember that System Restore will not make any difference to disks that only contain documents and standard file types. The important disk to tick is the

one that Windows and your program files are installed on.

7. Click **Create**.

8. Type an appropriate and memorable name for your restore point.

9. Click **Create**.

10. When the process is complete, click **OK**.

11. To close any open dialogs, keep clicking **Cancel**.

To backup the registry in Windows XP by setting a Manual System Restore Point:

1. Click **Start** > **All Programs** > **Accessories** > **System Tools** > **System Restore**.

2. Select **Create a Restore Point** and click **Next**.

3. Type a memorable name for your restore point.

4. Click **Create**.

5. Click **Close**.

■ **Windows 7 Annoyance: All My Windows Suddenly Disappear!**

Every so often, I think I must be jogging the mouse while I'm typing. At any rate, something causes it to spring to the bottom-right corner of the screen, where it lands on a tiny panel that causes the open windows on my screen to suddenly vanish. This is really getting on my nerves – is there any way to stop it?

This is a new feature of Windows 7 known as 'Aero Peek'. To the right of the taskbar, in the extreme bottom-right corner of the screen, there's a small rectangular panel, and when you move the mouse on to this panel, any open windows on your screen become see-through (apart from their borders) to let you see your desktop beneath them.

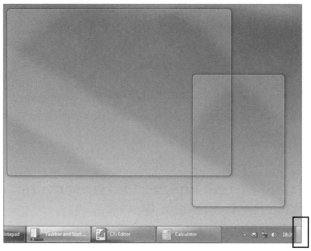

Aero Peek makes windows temporarily see-through

It's not an awfully useful feature even when you use it intentionally, but if the mouse pointer just lands there by accident while you're using one of those windows it can be extremely disconcerting! Fortunately, you can turn off this feature. Here's how:

1. Right-click the Start button and choose **Properties**.

2. In the dialog that appears, pictured in the next screenshot, switch to the **Taskbar** tab.

3. At the bottom of the dialog, remove the tick beside **Use Aero Peek to preview the desktop**.

4. Click **OK**.

From now on, if your mouse does happen to land on that little panel, nothing will happen.

Switch off Aero Peek to solve the problem

This tiny panel has a second use: if you click it, the windows on your screen will all be minimised, letting you see the desktop and its icons. When you've finished using the desktop, click the same little panel a second time and those windows will reappear. Even if you switch off the Aero Peek feature by following the steps above, you can still use this slightly-more-useful feature.

■ Vista Problem: I Can't Create New Contacts or Contact Groups

*When I open my 'Contacts' folder, I understand that I should see buttons labelled **New Contact** and **New Contact Group** on the green toolbar. For some reason they don't appear, so I can't create any new contacts. What's gone wrong?*

This is a common problem with Windows Vista. It's supposed to know (and remember) what kind of files are stored in particular folders, and show suitable buttons on the green toolbar according to which folder you've opened. In the case of your Contacts folder, Vista should know that this contains your contacts, and it should show buttons that allow you to add new contacts and contact groups.

Sadly, this feature just doesn't work very well: from time to time, you'll find that Vista has forgotten what your Contacts folder is for, and those handy buttons won't appear. When that happens, just follow these steps to put it right:

1. If your Contacts folder isn't already open, go to the Start menu and click your name, then double-click **Contacts** in the window that appears.

2. Right-click a blank white space in your Contacts folder (i.e. not on one of the files it contains).

3. On the menu that appears, click **Customize This Folder**.

4. Now you'll see the dialog pictured in the following screenshot, and the drop-down list near the top of the dialog probably says 'All Items' or 'Documents'. Open this drop-down list and choose **Contacts**.

Remind Windows Vista that this is your Contacts folder

5. Click **OK**. This dialog will close, returning you to your Contacts folder where you should see that those

New Contact and **New Contact Group** buttons now appear on the green toolbar.

■ How Can I Close a Program that's Stopped Working?

*A couple of programs I use have a tendency to 'freeze up' – clicks and key-presses don't do anything, and clicking the **x** button in their top-right corners to close them doesn't work. The only way I've found to close them is to restart the PC. Is there a less time-consuming way?*

The first point to make is that programs shouldn't freeze up like this; it usually indicates a bug (mistake) in the program, so it's often worth checking with the program's maker whether there's a newer version of the program available in which this bug is fixed.

Moving to the question, though, you certainly shouldn't have to restart your PC just to force a frozen program to close. Here's a much better way:

1. Right-click a blank space on the taskbar and choose **Task Manager** or **Start Task Manager**. (Alternatively, you can press the key combination **Ctrl+Shift+Esc**.)

2. In the Task Manager window that opens, select the **Applications** tab.

3. Here you'll see a list of all the programs currently running, one of which will be the program that has frozen. Alongside its name, under the 'Status' column, you'll probably see the words 'Not Responding', which confirms that the program really has frozen.

4. Click this program in the list, and then click the **End**

Task button at the bottom. (A dialog may now appear asking if you're sure you want to close the program, rather than waiting to see if it responds. Choose the option to close the program.)

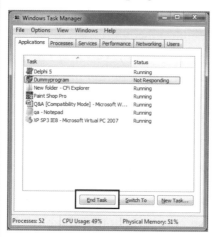

*Select the program to close and click **End Task***

5. It might take a few seconds for the frozen program to disappear from your screen (and from the list of programs in Task Manager). If it does, you're done and you can close the Task Manager window, ignoring the remaining steps below.

6. If the program still hasn't closed, continue following these steps.

7. Right-click the frozen program in the list, and choose **Go To Process**.

8. The Task Manager window will switch to its 'Processes' tab automatically and will select an item in the list on that page. Be careful not to click in this list or you'll select a different item and end up forcing some other program to close! If you think you might have clicked something different in the list, switch back to the **Applications** tab and repeat step 7.

9. At the bottom of the window, click **End Process**. At this point, a little dialog will appear asking if you're sure you want to terminate this process. (A 'process' is essentially just a technical name for a program.) In this little dialog, click **End process** in Windows 7/Vista, or **Yes** in Windows XP. This method rarely fails, and within a few seconds the frozen program should disappear from your screen, indicating that the program has been forced to close. You can then close the Task Manager window.

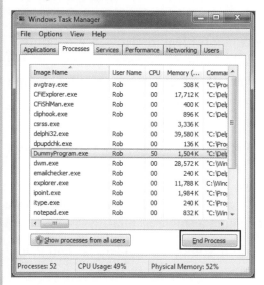

Force the misbehaving program to close

■ Vista Problem: My Files No Longer Have Names!

I have a strange problem in Windows Vista. When I open my 'Documents' folder, I can see icons for all my files, but they don't have names, so I can't tell which file is which any more! What's gone wrong?

You can see an example of this curiosity in the next screenshot: imagine opening a folder and seeing just a collection of icons like this with no names! How would you know which was the file or folder you were looking for?

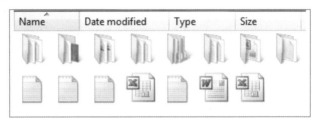

Without names, it's impossible to tell one item from another!

This can only happen in Windows Vista, and it's supposed to be a helpful feature. However, it's only meant to happen in folders containing pictures, on the basis that you can tell which file you want by looking at the picture. Even then, it should only happen if you specifically choose to hide the filenames.

Unfortunately, Windows Vista can get awfully confused about the way files should be displayed, and you can suddenly find that the filenames have vanished for no good reason – even in folders like the one shown above which doesn't contain a single picture!

Here's what to do if you open a folder and find that no filenames are shown:

1. Right-click a blank white space in the window (avoiding the icons) and choose **Customize This Folder**.

2. Before changing anything, make a mental note of what is currently shown in the drop-down list at the top of the dialog, because we'll choose the same option again a little later.

3. In the drop-down list choose **Pictures and Videos** (if that option isn't already selected). Make sure there isn't a tick in the checkbox below the list, then click **OK**.

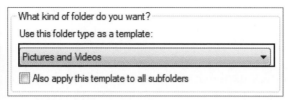

Tell Windows this folder contains pictures and videos (even if it doesn't!)

4. Now right-click a blank white space again, move the mouse to **View** and you'll see an item named 'Hide File Names' which will have a tick beside it. Click **Hide File Names** to remove the tick and turn off the option to hide filenames.

Force Windows to display file names once more

5. I asked you to make a mental note of what was shown in the drop-down list in step 2. If it already said 'Pictures and Videos', you can skip this step. If it said something different, right-click a blank white space in the window, choose **Customize This Folder** and set the drop-down list back to the option you found selected in step 2. Once again, make sure there's no tick in the checkbox below the list and click **OK**.

The icons in this folder should now look just the way they did before, but their filenames will now be displayed.

Here's a quick explanation of what we've had to do. Although step 4 is the important step that makes Windows display the filenames, we first have to tell Windows that this folder contains pictures and videos (even if it doesn't), otherwise this vital **Hide File Names** option isn't displayed. Once we've done that, and followed step 4 to reveal the filenames, we go back and tell Windows that the folder contains whatever it really does contain.

■ Why Have All My Desktop Icons Disappeared?

Until a couple of days ago I had a variety of icons on my desktop. Now, for some reason, the desktop is completely empty: my background wallpaper is still there, but there's not an icon in sight! What's happened?

This shouldn't happen spontaneously, but it's something you might do accidentally (or someone else using your computer may think it an amusing way to wind you up!), and it can cause a lot of head-scratching if you're not aware that this peculiar option exists!

The culprit is a setting in Windows 7, Vista and XP that allows you to hide all the icons on your desktop, giving you a more attractive view of your wallpaper without any icons cluttering it up.

With two clicks you can hide all the icons on your desktop

To make your desktop icons visible again, follow these steps:

1. Right-click a blank space on your desktop (which, as you can't see any icons, can be absolutely anywhere!).

2. Move the mouse to **View** in Windows 7/Vista, or **Arrange Icons By** in Windows XP, and a little submenu will pop open.

3. Near the bottom of the submenu you'll see an item labelled **Show Desktop Icons**. Normally this should have a tick beside it, indicating that desktop icons are being shown. At the moment, of course, it won't. Click on **Show Desktop Icons**: this replaces the tick beside it and your icons will reappear.

Of course, if you want to hide your desktop icons, you can follow the same steps. This time you'll be removing the tick beside **Show Desktop Icons** which makes the icons disappear. Just remember that that's what you've done, so you'll know how to get them back again!

■ How to Get Old Programs Working in Windows 7 or Vista

I recently bought a new PC running Windows 7 and installed my usual programs on it. However, one of those programs refuses to work properly. When I start it, it shows an error message, flashes on to the screen very briefly and then closes. Is there any way to get it working?

You should find that any program that worked in Windows Vista will work in Windows 7, and the majority of programs that were written in the time of Windows XP can also still be used in Windows 7/Vista. However, some XP-era programs (and many that were written for earlier versions of Windows) might be reluctant to run in Windows 7/Vista.

Fortunately, both Windows 7 and Vista have a useful feature named 'Compatibility Mode' which may be able to solve the problem. Essentially, this fools the program into believing it's running on an older version of Windows, and in many cases this simple bit of trickery will be enough to coax the program into running normally.

To try this trick for a program that won't otherwise run correctly in Windows 7/Vista, follow these steps:

1. Open the Start menu and find your way to the item you would normally click to start the misbehaving program.

2. Rather than clicking the item in the normal way, right-click it instead, and then choose **Properties** from the menu that opens.

3. In the dialog that appears, select the **Compatibility** tab and you'll see the options pictured in the next screenshot.

4. Tick the box beside **Run this program in compatibility mode for**.

5. In the drop-down list immediately below, select the version of Windows you were using previously – in other words, a version of Windows in which you know this program runs correctly.

You'll notice that some versions of Windows are listed several times with 'Service Pack' numbers beside them. If you were in the habit of keeping your old PC up-to-date, choose the highest of the Service Pack numbers. For example, if you used Windows XP, you'd choose **Windows XP (Service Pack 3)**.

6. Click the **OK** button at the bottom of the dialog to save the changes and close the dialog.

7. Now open the Start menu again, find and click the item that starts your misbehaving program, and see if it now runs correctly. Assuming it does, you've finished and you can ignore the remaining steps.

8. If the program still doesn't run correctly, follow steps 1–3 again and try the following:

- If you're not sure you picked the correct version of Windows in step 5, try choosing a slightly earlier version – for example, **Windows XP (Service Pack 2)**. Click **OK** then try running your program to see if that has made the difference.

- Near the bottom of the dialog, tick the box beside **Run this program as an administrator**, then click **OK** and try running your program. With this setting, you'll see a security warning headed 'User Account Control' each time you start the program, and you'll have to click **Yes** or **Allow** to allow the program to start.

■ Vista Problem: Windows Media Player Won't Start!

I'm using Windows Vista, and although I know Windows Media Player is installed, I can rarely start it. Sometimes it does open, but more often than not nothing happens at all! What's going on?

This seems to be an unusual bug (mistake) in Windows Vista that affects some Vista users, but not all. I haven't heard a sensible reason put forward for it, nor a conclusive fix. However, I can explain what's happening and what you can do when you try to start Windows Media Player and nothing happens.

Unlike most other programs, Windows Media Player is designed in such a way that you can only have one instance of it open at a time. In other words, if it's already running and you go to your Start menu and try to start it, you won't get a second Media Player window, you'll just be ignored.

What's happening to the questioner (and other Vista users) is that Windows Media Player starts of its own accord for some reason, but completely invisibly: its window doesn't appear on the screen and there's no sign that it's running. However, when you try to start it, the system spots that it's already running, this 'only one instance' rule kicks in and you're ignored.

When this happens, the solution is to stop the invisible Windows Media Player that's already running by following these steps:

1. Press **Ctrl+Shift+Esc** which opens a window headed Windows Task Manager, pictured in the next screenshot.
2. Select the **Processes** tab.
3. Look down the alphabetical list to find **wmplayer.exe** and select it.
4. Click the **End Process** button.

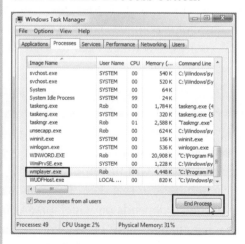

Force the hidden Media Player to close

5. A dialog will appear asking if you're sure about this and warning of potential problems. In this particular case (and only this one!) you can ignore the warning, so click the **End process** button in this dialog to confirm that you really do want to 'end this process'

as the terminology has it.

6. Close the Windows Task Manager window. You've now closed that hidden instance of Windows Media Player, so you'll now be able to start it successfully.

■ Is It Really Safe to Use System Restore?

On many occasions I've used System Restore to solve problems with my PC, but today after doing so again I started getting error messages every few minutes. I reversed the System Restore I had done, which seems to have stopped the errors, but this has left me wondering whether System Restore is as reliable as I thought it was.

In case you're not aware of it, System Restore is a feature built into Windows 7, Vista and XP. It takes regular 'snapshots' of your system's setup and stores them, along with the date each snapshot was made. You can use System Restore to switch all your PC's settings back to what they were on one of those earlier dates.

Using System Restore to roll back your system this way certainly can be risky though. This isn't because System Restore is unreliable – quite the reverse: it does a very thorough job. Any settings or system files that weren't on your PC at the date you choose will be removed or disabled when you switch back to that date. This may have no ill effects at all, but much depends on which date you switch back to, and what changes have been made to your PC since then. If you've installed or updated any software or hardware, for example, it's possible that it will no longer work properly.

Although it's comforting to know that System Restore is there, it really isn't intended to be used to fix minor niggles! Treat it as a last resort for times when something serious has gone wrong and you can't find any other solution for the problem, not as your first port of call.

Because System Restore can potentially leave you with more problems than you started with, it takes a snapshot of your system as it is now before restoring it to an earlier date. Keep this in mind, because it allows you to undo the System Restore it just performed if things have been made worse.

■ My Taskbar Has Moved to the Side of the Screen!

I'm not sure what has caused this, but the taskbar that should be running along the bottom of my screen has jumped to the right! How can I put it back where it's supposed to be?

You may be surprised to learn that the taskbar isn't actually 'supposed to be' at the bottom of the screen. That's where most of us have it, but it can be at any of the other three edges and some people much prefer it at the top, left or right.

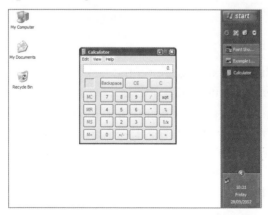

You can place the taskbar at any edge of the screen

This obviously means that the taskbar can be moved around, which means that it could be moved accidentally. If you suddenly find that your taskbar is sitting along a different edge of the screen from the edge you'd prefer, follow the appropriate steps below to move it back again:

Windows 7:

1. Right-click a blank space on the taskbar (a space not occupied by a button or icon) and choose **Properties**.

2. In the dialog that appears, open the drop-down list labelled **Taskbar location on screen** and choose **Bottom** (or, of course, whichever edge of the screen you prefer).

3. Click **OK**.

Windows Vista/XP:

1. Right-click a blank space on the taskbar (a space containing no buttons, icons or text).

2. Near the bottom of the menu that appears, look for an item that says **Lock the Taskbar**. If there's a tick beside this item, this means your taskbar is locked and can't be moved: click **Lock the Taskbar** to unlock it.

The taskbar must be 'unlocked' before you can move it elsewhere

3. Once again, find a blank space on the taskbar, press the left mouse button and hold it down.

4. Now, keeping the left mouse button down, drag the mouse to the edge of the screen where you want the taskbar to be placed. Don't worry that nothing seems to be happening when you drag the mouse, just keep going. When you get close enough to the edge of the screen, the taskbar will suddenly jump from its current position to the edge you want. When it does, you can release the mouse button.

5. Finally, it's a good idea to lock the taskbar into its new position. This prevents anyone who uses your computer from dragging it to a different position. Once again, right-click a blank space on the taskbar and click **Lock the Taskbar**.

■ Where is the 'Run' Command in Windows 7/Vista?

I'm trying to follow some steps I found on a web page which were supposed to work in Windows Vista, but I've fallen at the first hurdle: it says to

> *choose **Start** > **Run**, and there's no Run option on Vista's Start menu!*

Microsoft has done some tidying-up in Windows 7 and Vista, and the Run command was one of the casualties. It no longer appears on the Start menu, presumably because it isn't used often enough to deserve such a privileged position.

When you do need it, you can still open it from the keyboard by pressing **Win+R** (the Windows key, two to the left of the space bar, along with the 'R' key), as you can in all earlier versions of Windows. You can also reach it by going to **Start** > **All Programs** > **Accessories** > **Run**.

If you'd like to see the Run item in its more-familiar place at the right of your Start menu, there's a quick tweak you can make to put it back there. Just follow these steps:

1. Right-click the Start button and choose **Properties**.

2. A dialog will appear containing several tabs. Make sure the **Start Menu** tab is selected, as shown in the next screenshot, and click the **Customize** button.

3. Now another dialog will appear, pictured in the

following screenshot. In the list at the top of this dialog, scroll downwards until you see the **Run command** item.

4. Click the **Run command** item to put a tick in the box to its left.

5. Finally, click **OK** in the dialog you're using, and **OK** again in the dialog you opened in step 1.

Now, if you open the Start menu, you'll find the Run command nestling near the bottom on the right-hand side.

If you decide later that you'd like to remove the Run command from the Start menu, follow the same set of steps again, but remove the tick you added beside **Run command** in step 4.

■ Windows 7: Why Do Windows Jump to the Top or Side of the Screen when Moved?

When I try to move a window around my screen in Windows 7, the window has a habit of jumping to one edge of the screen and resizing itself. Can I stop it doing that?

This is a new feature in Windows 7, and it's supposed to be helpful. If you drag a window up to the top of your screen, it will maximise itself to fill your entire screen. If you drag a window to the left or right edges, it will jump to that edge and resize itself to fill half your screen's width – you can then drag a different window to the opposite edge, making it do the same and allowing you to compare the two windows side by side.

Although this might seem like annoying behaviour, you do have some control over it. If you don't want the window to jump to a particular edge of the screen like this, don't let go of the mouse button when it happens, but just keep dragging the window to where you want it. Or, if it caught you by surprise and you did release the mouse button, just drag the window away from that edge again and move it to where you want it.

However, if you find this feature truly annoying, you can turn it off. Here's how:

1. Open the Start menu and click **Control Panel**.

2. In the Control Panel window, click the green words **Ease of Access**.

3. Next, below the 'Ease of Access Center' heading, click the smaller blue words **Change how your mouse works**.

4. Near the bottom of the window you'll find an option labelled **Prevent windows from being**

automatically arranged when moved to the edge of the screen. Tick the box beside this option, then click the **OK** button at the bottom and close the Control Panel window.

If you decide you miss this Windows 7 feature after all and want to turn it back on, just follow the same steps again, but remove the tick you added in step 4.

■ Have I Been Scammed Over the Software On My New PC?

A few months ago I bought a new PC which came with some software pre-installed, including Microsoft Office 2010 and BullGuard Internet Security. Without warning, a few weeks ago, Microsoft Office announced that it had expired after 25 uses and that I had to purchase a copy. I've since discovered that my BullGuard Internet Security is about to expire after 90 days. Am I right in thinking this is a scam by the company that sold me the PC?

In the vast majority of cases the answer is 'No', but the real test is what you were told about the software being supplied with your PC.

Almost all new PCs come with some extra software installed, besides Windows itself. Some of those programs will be 'full' versions which are yours to use forever, while others will be 'trial' versions designed to work normally for two or three months (or to be used only a set number of times) and then expire, preventing you from using them unless you pay for them. (As you can probably guess, the point of these trials is that you become so used to using the software that, as the trial comes to an end, you feel you can't live without it and will decide to pay for it. Of course, rather than paying, you may prefer just to uninstall it and use something different instead.)

Now, you may find some software on your new PC that you weren't expecting – it wasn't mentioned in any advertising or literature. If that turns out to be trial software, you can't really complain, because you weren't expecting to receive it anyway.

If the software you were expecting turns out to be trial software, check the details you were given about it when you ordered the PC. If there was nothing to suggest that it was a trial (or, particularly, if it was said to be a 'full' version), you may have grounds for complaint. Even more importantly, if you paid an additional amount to have this software, you most certainly shouldn't have received a trial version.

The two software programs mentioned in the question, Microsoft Office and BullGuard Internet Security, are frequently included as trial copies on new PCs: very rarely would you receive a full copy of either without paying extra for it. It's most likely that both were noted as being trial copies in the details of the PC, but perhaps in small print that wasn't very noticeable.

When it comes to software, the only thing you can be sure of getting with a new PC is a copy of Windows installed. Beyond that, you may get nothing at all, or you may get quite a lot, but some of what you get may be trial software. Before you order or pay for the PC, be sure to check all the details carefully so that you know exactly what you're getting for your money!

Chapter 6

Solve Windows Error Messages Fast

"Whenever I see an error message on my PC, I panic. What do I do to fix them?"

■ Error: Not a Valid Win32 Application

I have just downloaded a program from the Internet and double-clicked it to begin installing it. As soon as I double-click I see an error message that says 'Not a valid Win32 application.' What does this mean?

This isn't an error message you should see very often, and in almost every case you'll only see it in the circumstances mentioned in the question: when you've downloaded a program from a website and you've double-clicked it to start installing it.

The error message means that the program file you've downloaded is incomplete. For some reason, the website sent you the beginning of the file – and perhaps quite a large chunk of it – but something went wrong: the website stopped sending any more of the file and instead reported to your system that the download was complete.

Programs are designed in such a way that Windows can tell whether there is a piece missing before it runs the program. Since running an incomplete program could cause problems, Windows displays the error message referred to in the question (which in everyday language means 'There's a problem with this program that prevents Windows from starting it') and makes no attempt to get the program running.

As the program you've downloaded is no use for anything, the first thing to do is to delete it. Having done that, return to the web page from which you downloaded it and try downloading it again. In the majority of cases, the hiccup that occurred the first time won't be repeated and you'll receive a complete copy of the program which will start successfully when you double-click it.

If the same thing happens this time as well, it suggests that something more fundamental has gone wrong, but not at your end. You could try deleting the file again and downloading the program a third time, but whether you fancy doing that depends on the size of the file, the speed of your Internet connection, and your patience!

After two failures, and certainly after three, you can assume that the problem is more than just a little hiccup in the downloading process. It's almost certain that the problem is with the website itself, and that everyone who tries to download the program also receives an incomplete file.

If you're really keen to get a copy of the program, there are two options. The first is to go back to the website and see if they provide a link to download the file from a different website (known as a 'mirror'), on the basis that this alternative copy should download successfully. Alternatively, contact the website owner to explain what's happening each time you download the program and ask them to check whether there's a problem with it at their end. (There almost certainly is, but it's best to be diplomatic when asking!)

■ What is the 'Thumbs.db' File I'm Being Warned About Deleting?

I've just deleted a folder of pictures and I was asked if I was sure I wanted to delete 'thumbs.db' which was said to be a system file. I said 'No', the folder is still there (but minus the pictures it contained) and there are no files at all inside it. It seems that this 'thumbs.db' file was deleted anyway! What's going on?

When you open a folder containing pictures in recent versions of Windows, you see small versions (known as 'thumbnails') of the pictures themselves. It takes Windows a little time to examine each picture file and generate these small versions, so when it's done this the first time it stores these thumbnails in a database file named 'thumbs.db'. This file is hidden, so you can't see it among your pictures, but Windows will use it next time you open the folder to display the thumbnails far quicker.

If you delete that folder, you'll also be deleting its 'thumbs.db' file but – for some reason – Windows chooses to ask your permission first. If you say no, as the questioner did, all the pictures will be deleted but the folder itself will be left behind with the 'thumbs.db' file still inside it. However, as it's hidden, you can't see it and the folder appears to be empty! Silly, isn't it?

In fact, it's always safe to say 'Yes' to this question and allow the 'thumbs.db' file to be deleted. If all the pictures themselves are being deleted, that 'thumbs.db' file is of no use anyway. And, even if you somehow managed to delete the 'thumbs.db' file by itself, Windows would recreate it next time you opened the folder to look at its pictures.

■ Error: The Print Spooler Service is Not Running

I switched my computer on this morning and the printer won't work! I've checked all the connections and the printer's power light is on, but when I try to print something I just get a message saying that the print spooler service is not running. What does that mean?

The 'print spooler' is a vital part of Windows that enables you to print things, keeping track of what's waiting to be printed and handling the job of feeding the data to your printer. Whenever you try to print something, the print spooler is given all the relevant details and left to get on with the job while you (and your computer) do other things.

The print spooler should therefore be running all the time in case it's needed, but occasionally something goes haywire: either the print spooler doesn't start when you switch on your computer or something causes it to stop. Usually the first you'll know about this is when you try to print something and an error message appears telling you that the print spooler service is not running.

If this happens, don't try printing a second time! Your document has already been prepared for printing, but it can't yet be sent to your printer. If you try a second time, you'll get the same error message again, and a second copy of the same document will be scheduled for printing (which you probably don't want!).

Instead, follow these steps to get that print spooler running again:

1. Right-click the **Computer** or **My Computer** icon on your Start menu or desktop and choose **Manage**.

2. In the left-hand section of the 'Computer Management' window that opens (pictured in the next screenshot), click the arrowhead or **+** sign beside **Services and Applications**, and then click on **Services**.

3. In the main section of the window to the right you'll now see a long alphabetical list of items. Scroll down this list to find the item named **Print Spooler**.

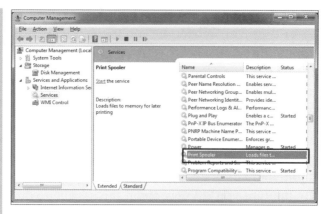

4. Double-click the **Print Spooler** item, or, if you prefer, right-click the item and choose **Properties**.

5. Now you'll see the dialog pictured in the next screenshot. About halfway down, alongside the words 'Startup type' you'll see a drop-down list. Make sure this drop-down list shows **Automatic**. (If it doesn't, open the drop-down list and choose **Automatic** from it.)

6. A little further down you'll see a row of four buttons. Click the button labelled **Start**.

7. You'll briefly see another small dialog indicating that Windows is starting this 'print spooler service'. When that disappears, click **OK** and then close the Computer Management window. Within a few seconds, the document waiting to be printed should be sent to your printer, and any further documents you try to print will also be printed without any arguments.

■ Internet Explorer Keeps Saying There Are Errors on the Page

At quite a few of the websites I visit in Internet Explorer, a note appears at the bottom of the window saying 'Done, but with errors on page'. Should I be worried about this?

Ordinarily, when a web page has finished loading, you should see the word 'Done' in the bottom-left corner of Internet Explorer. However, sometimes you'll see the note shown in the following screenshot, accompanied by an exclamation-mark symbol.

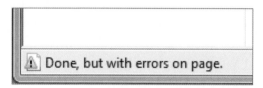

The simple answer to the question is: no, there's absolutely nothing to be concerned about. It just means that the web page's designer made one or more mistakes in the code of the page, and that some aspects of the page may not appear (or work) quite as they should. However, those mistakes will rarely make any noticeable difference to the page. (In old versions of Internet Explorer, these errors would pop up in separate boxes, not only alerting you to things that didn't matter, but forcing you to click **OK** to them all before you could read the page. At least this little note can be easily ignored!)

■ Windows 7: Fix the STOP 0x0000007B Error Caused by a Faulty Hard Disk Setting

I read that to make the most of my PC's SATA hard disk I should enable AHCI in the BIOS. When I tried this, I got a blue screen error from Windows 7 as soon as I restarted and couldn't get any further. Was this advice wrong or is something else needed?

If your PC uses a Serial ATA (SATA) type hard drive, as most new PCs do, you may find that Windows 7 refuses to boot if you change the mode of the drive in the BIOS, setting it to use the Advanced Host Controller Interface (AHCI) specification. When you try to startup Windows you will see the error message:

STOP 0x0000007B INACCESSABLE_BOOT_DEVICE

To fix this problem, you need to enable the AHCI driver in Windows before changing the mode of the SATA driver. First, change back the setting of the drive in the BIOS, then start Windows normally. Next, backup the registry, then enable the driver as follows:

1. Press **Windows Key + R,** type **REGEDIT** and click **OK**.
2. Navigate to the registry key: HKEY_LOCAL_MACHINE\System\CurrentControl Set\Services\Msahci
3. In the right-hand panel, right-click on **Start** and then click **Modify**.
4. Change the **Value data** box to **0** to enable the driver.
5. Click **OK** and close the Registry Editor.

With the driver enabled, you can change your drive configuration back in the BIOS.

■ **Fix Error 4201 when Trying to Start the Windows Event Viewer**

I'm trying to get to the bottom of a problem with my PC and I'm advised that the Windows Event

Viewer should give me some useful clues. However, when I try to open the Event Viewer it fails to start and gives error 4201. How can I fix this?

The Windows Event Viewer is an essential troubleshooting tool. It contains details of practically every operation that Windows carries out, so it should be your first port of call when trying to track down PC errors. Unfortunately, the Event Viewer relies on a service named the Windows Event service which itself is susceptible to errors, and since it isn't running, it can be difficult to find out what those errors are. If you come across error 4201 when the Windows Event Log service is started or when you try to open the Event Viewer, the problem is probably due to incorrect file permissions on a file required by the Event Log service. To resolve the problem, follow these steps:

1. Reboot the computer and begin pressing the **F8** key repeatedly, about twice a second, as the PC is restarting.

2. When the Advanced Options menu is displayed, use the up or down arrow keys to select **Safe Mode**, then press **Enter**.

3. Once Windows starts in Safe Mode, open Windows Explorer and navigate to:
   C:\Windows\System32\LogFiles\WMI

4. Right-click on the **RtBackup** folder and choose **Properties**.

5. Click the **Security** tab, and then click the **Continue** button in Windows 7/Vista or the **Edit** button in Windows XP.

6. Click **Add**.

7. Type **SYSTEM** and press **Enter**.

8. Tick **Allow** next to the **Full control** option.

9. Click **OK**, and then click **Yes**.

10. Restart the computer and the Event Log service should have automatically started up, allowing you to open the Event Viewer.

■ How Do I get Rid of Error 2 when Starting Windows Firewall?

When I try to start the Windows Firewall in Windows XP SP2, I see an error message reporting that the firewall could not be started, along with error code 2. What does this mean and how can I fix it?

This problem happens when one of two crucial files is missing from your system: IPNATHLP.DLL or IPNAT.SYS. To resolve the problem, you need to replace the appropriate file with a fresh copy from your Windows XP installation CD.

To do so, first insert your XP installation CD into your CD-ROM/DVD drive, then proceed as follows:

1. Click **Start > Run**, type **CMD** and click **OK**.

2. At the command prompt, type: **expand X:\i386\ipnathlp.dl_ %systemroot%\system32\ipnat hlp.dll** and press **Enter**. Replace the letter X with the letter of your CD-ROM drive in My Computer.

3. Next type **expand X:\i386\ipnat.sy_ %systemroot %\system32\drivers\ipnat.sys** and press **Enter**. Again, replace X with the letter of your CD-ROM drive.

4. Type **EXIT** followed by **Enter** then restart your PC for the changes to take effect.

■ **Windows 7: Help! System Restore Point Error 0x80070032 Prevents Me from Creating a Restore Point?**

Whenever I try to create a System Restore point in Windows Vista, I get the error code 0x80070032 and find that I'm not able to create the restore point. Can you help prevent this error?

This happens when the Windows Event Log service and the Task Scheduler service (both of which System Restore depends on) are disabled. To fix the problem, follow these steps:

1. Click **Start**, type **Services.msc** and press **Enter**.
2. Double-click **Windows Event Log**.
3. In the Start type list box, ensure that **Automatic** is selected.
4. Click **Start** to start the service, if it's not already running.
5. Double-click **Task Scheduler**.
6. In the Start type list box, ensure that **Automatic** is selected.
7. Click **Start** to start the service, if it's not already running.
8. Close the Services console.
9. Restart Windows.

■ **Internet: What Does 'HTTP Error 500' Mean?**

I just tried to visit a web page I've used many times, and my browser displayed the message 'HTTP Error 500: Internal server error' in large black text on an otherwise-blank page. What does that mean?

Let's start with the 'HTTP' bit. This is the name of a kind of computer language that makes the World Wide Web work. You've probably noticed that all web addresses begin 'http://', and – in very simple terms – that's to tell all the computers involved that they need to use this HTTP language to make sense of the address that follows.

When you try to visit a web page, your computer sends a request for the page to the computer (or 'server') that stores it. If all goes well, that server will send back the page to be displayed. Whatever happens, the server will also send back an 'error number' to your PC telling it the result of the request. Usually that number will be 200, which means 'Everything went swimmingly and I'm sending you the page.' (In this case, then, it's an error number that indicates there were no errors!)

There are all sorts of numbers that could be sent back, but let's focus on 500, the error number in the question. The error numbers in the 500s all mean that the server itself has done something wrong. Number 500 itself is the most basic one, meaning that the server got itself confused in some unspecified way and couldn't send you the web page.

The vast majority of these errors are not your problem, rather refreshingly – you've done nothing to cause them, and there's nothing much you can do about them. It's always worth pressing the **F5** key on your keyboard if you see one of these numeric errors: this tells your browser to request the same page again. In the case of the 500 errors, another attempt may well succeed. If it doesn't, it's still worth trying again in a few minutes, or tomorrow, in the hope that the server has started behaving itself again.

Chapter 7

Get Rid of Annoying Email Problems for Optimal Use

"I thought email was supposed to be easy to use, but irritating problems keep cropping up. Can you help?"

■ Email Error: The Host Could Not be Found

Whenever I send and receive email, I get an error message that says 'The host Tiscali could not be found'. How can I get my email working?

This error message rattles on for a few more lines, including some rather technical-looking details, but the first line, quoted above, is the one that matters.

When you get this error message, you may find that you're unable to send or to receive any email. Alternatively, you could find that messages can be sent but not received, or vice versa.

This error message usually indicates that there's a mistake in your email settings, but it may simply be that your ISP's computer is temporarily out of action. If you don't think any settings have been changed on your PC, it's a good idea to wait an hour or so and try again just in case it was a fault at your ISP's end.

If you're continuing to get the same error, the reason will be that you've made a mistake in typing the name of your ISP's computer in your email settings. There are actually two computers involved (which are more correctly known as 'servers'), one used when you send mail and the other used when you receive. If either of these servers' names was typed wrongly, your email program won't be able to connect to it, and the error message will appear.

To check and correct the names of these servers, follow these steps in Windows Mail or Outlook Express:

1. First, check the correct names of your ISP's email servers. You should be able to find these among the paperwork your ISP sent you, or in the Help or

Support section of their website, or by giving them a ring. One of these servers is known as an 'SMTP server' and the other as a 'POP3 server'. (The first of these sends email and the second receives it. You may find that both have the same name.)

2. In your email program, choose **Tools** > **Accounts**.

3. In the 'Mail' section, select the email account you're having trouble with and then click the **Properties** button.

4. Another dialog will appear: select the **Servers** tab.

5. Near the top you'll see two text boxes labelled **Incoming mail (POP3)** and **Outgoing mail (SMTP)**. The text in these boxes must exactly match the names of your ISP's servers. If either is incorrect, delete the text shown in the box and then carefully type the correct name. The name of the POP3 server goes in the **Incoming mail** box, and the name of the SMTP server in the **Outgoing mail** box.

My incoming mail server is a	POP3	server.
Incoming mail (POP3):	pop.myisp.co.uk	
Outgoing mail (SMTP):	smtp.myisp.co.uk	

Type the correct server names into the two boxes

6. Double-check what you've typed to ensure the names really are correct (that the dots really are dots and not commas, that no spaces are included, and so on).

7. Click **OK** and then close the Internet Accounts window. If you now try sending and receiving email, you should find that the process goes without a hitch and no error message appears.

■ Error Sending Email: 'Some of the Files Could Not Be Found'

I just attached a Microsoft Word document to an email message and tried to send it, but received an error saying that some of the files could not be found. I've attached files many times before without problems, so what could the problem be this time?

This is a problem you could run into when trying to send a Word document or an Excel spreadsheet using Windows Mail in Windows Vista. Although you know you've attached the file correctly and can see it listed in the 'Attachments' section at the top of the message, when you click Send you see this error:

> Some of the files could not be found, and could not be attached to the message. Would you like to send the message anyway?

The actual cause of the problem isn't that the file can't be found, but that it's still open in Microsoft Word or Excel. Click **No** in this error message, and then close Word or Excel, saving the file along the way if necessary. After doing that, you should be able to send the email message successfully.

■ Email Messages I Send Don't Go into the Outbox

When I send an email message from my new PC, it doesn't get put into the Outbox, but goes straight into the Sent Items folder. Can this be changed?

You can choose whether or not the Outbox is used in Microsoft email programs. If it isn't, messages will be sent as soon as you click their **Send** button after writing them; if it is, messages won't be sent until you click the **Send/Receive** button, giving you a chance to open the Outbox and reopen a message to edit it before you send it (or, indeed, to delete it if you've changed your mind about sending it).

To find this option in Windows Live Mail, click the blue tab at the far left of the Ribbon and choose **Options** > **Mail**. In Windows Mail or Outlook Express, go to **Tools** > **Options**. Select the **Send** tab in the dialog that appears, and you'll see an option labelled **Send messages immediately**. Remove the tick from this option if you'd like the Outbox to be used, and then click **OK**.

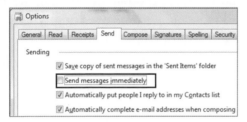

Ensure the Outbox is being used in your email program

■ Windows Mail Says It Can't Check My Spelling!

I've just tried to check the spelling of an email message in Windows Mail and I received an error message saying 'This language is no longer available for spell checking. Please select another in the spelling options dialog.' Does this really mean that English spelling can't be checked?

Although that certainly does seem to be the implication of the error message, it's not actually the case. (It would be a bizarre oversight for an American company to forget to include an English spell checker!) In fact, it's due to a bug (mistake) in Windows Mail, and it's a quick and easy one to fix.

To get your English spell checker working in Windows Mail, click **OK** in the message above if it's still on your screen and then follow these steps:

1. First, switch to the main Windows Mail window by clicking its button on the taskbar. (There's no need to close the email message you were writing: you'll be able to return to it after completing these steps.)

2. In that main window, open the **Tools** menu and click **Options**.

3. In the dialog that appears, select the **Spelling** tab, pictured in the following screenshot.

4. In the 'Language' section at the bottom of the dialog, you'll notice that 'English' is already selected in the drop-down list. That's the bug in Windows Mail that we need to fix: although it seems that the spell checker is already set to use English, behind the scenes Windows Mail apparently thinks no language at all has been selected, which is why it tells you that it's not available.

5. Start by opening that drop-down list and choosing one of the other languages – French, German or Spanish, it doesn't matter which as long as you don't choose English.

6. Click the **Apply** button at the bottom of the dialog.

7. Now open that drop-down list again, and this time

choose **English**.

8. Click **Apply** once again, and then click **OK** to confirm the change and close this dialog.

Switch to a language other than English first, then select English

If you now switch back to the email message you were writing (by clicking its button on the taskbar) and choose **Tools > Spelling** or press the **F7** key, you'll find that Windows Mail now cheerfully checks your spelling.

The one drawback to Windows Mail's spell checker is that it uses American English rather than British English. For this, unfortunately, there's no workaround, so be prepared to be told that words like 'colour', 'cheque' and 'licence' are spelt wrongly and click the **Ignore All** button!

■ Outlook Express Says a Recipient was Rejected by the Server

*Some time ago, when I tried to send an email message, Outlook Express said it could not be sent because one of the recipients was rejected by the server. Since then, every time I click **Send/Receive**, I see exactly the same error message! How can I stop this happening?*

The reason why the error message appeared the very first time is that there was a mistake in the email address to which the message was being sent. It would have been a simple typing mistake: perhaps the @ sign was missed out of the address, or a comma was typed in place of a dot, or the address contained a space. Whatever the exact mistake, it meant that this email address couldn't possibly exist, so Outlook Express didn't try to send it and displayed the error message instead.

That explains the original error message, but why does it keep reappearing? Well, if the message can't be sent, Outlook Express leaves it in the Outbox. It doesn't delete the message, and if it moved the message into the Sent Items folder that would give you the mistaken impression the message had been sent after all.

If you leave this message in the Outbox, Outlook Express will try to send it every time you click the **Send/Receive** button. Of course, the email address in the message still contains the same mistake, so Outlook Express will find the same problem with it each time and display the same error message!

Here's the solution – in fact, there is a choice of two solutions:

- One option is simply to delete the message so that

Outlook Express won't keep trying to send it. Click the **Outbox** folder to see its contents, then click this message once to select it and press the **Delete** key on your keyboard.

• Alternatively, you can open the message, correct the mistake in the email address and send it again. Click the **Outbox** folder, double-click the message to open it, and then edit the address shown in the **To** field. When you're sure the address is correct, click **Send**. This will replace the old message in the Outbox with this edited copy. When you click **Send/Receive**, Outlook Express will again try to send this message and, assuming the address is now valid, it should succeed.

■ Pictures in Email Messages are Replaced with a Small Red Cross

In some of the email messages I receive, the places where pictures are supposed to appear are replaced with an empty box containing a small red cross in the top-right corner. How can I make the pictures appear?

The red cross basically means that the pictures are not available to be shown. There are two possible reasons for this, and the most usual is that Windows Mail or Outlook Express (whichever you're using) has blocked them for security reasons.

Why would your email program do that? Well, rather than include the pictures in the email message itself, the sender placed them on a website and only included links to those pictures in the message. (This is common practice in newsletter-type messages sent to many people.) The links to those pictures could be designed to identify which recipients collected the pictures, thus letting the sender know who actually received and read the email message. On the off-chance that the message was sent by somebody who was up to no good, Windows Mail and Outlook Express ignore these links to pictures and simply replace the pictures with a box and a red cross.

If this happens to you, look further up the message window, just below the 'Subject' line, and you should see these words:

Some pictures have been blocked to help prevent the sender from identifying your computer. Click here to download pictures.

If the message is from someone you know and trust, click the yellow or grey block containing those words. Your email program will then fetch the pictures and display them in the correct positions in the message.

Click the coloured bar above the message if you want to see the pictures

I mentioned there were two possible reasons, and the second is that the sender's email settings may be incorrect, preventing the pictures he was trying to send from actually being included. Contact the sender to explain that the pictures were missing and suggest following these steps to solve the problem (which, of course, you can follow yourself if you discover that the pictures you're trying to send are not arriving):

1. In Windows Mail or Outlook Express, choose **Tools > Options** and select the **Send** tab.
2. In the **Mail Sending Format** section, click the **HTML Settings** button.
3. Tick the box beside **Send pictures with messages**.
4. Click **OK** to confirm this change, then **OK** again in the Options dialog.

■ How to Transfer Email Messages to a New PC

I've just bought a new PC and copied my files to it from the old one. The thing that has me foxed is email: where can I find my email messages to copy those to the new computer?

Assuming you're using either Windows Mail or Outlook Express on the old PC, it's not quite as straightforward as copying your other files – your documents, pictures, music and so on. Both of these email programs tuck your email away in a folder that you'd never stumble upon by accident and, once you've found it, the routine isn't quite the same as copying your other files.

Let's start with the steps for finding out where your email is stored on your old PC. For this I'll assume that you've been using either Windows Mail or Outlook Express on the old PC:

1. Start Windows Mail or Outlook Express and choose **Tools > Options**.
2. In the Options dialog that appears, do the following:

- In Windows Mail, select the **Advanced** tab, then click the **Maintenance** button, and then click the **Store Folder** button.
- In Outlook Express, select the **Maintenance** tab and then click the **Store Folder** button.

3. Now you'll see the little 'Store Location' dialog pictured in the following screenshot. This tells you the path to the folder containing your email messages. Right-click in the box showing this path and choose **Select All**. This will highlight all the text in that box (usually in blue).

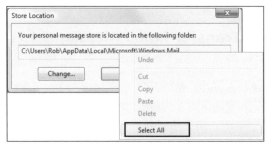

4. Now right-click inside the same box again and this time choose **Copy**. You won't see anything interesting happen, but we've accomplished the first step. Click **Cancel** in this little dialog, then either **Close** or **Cancel** in the dialogs you opened to reach this point, and finally close your email program.

5. The next step is to open the 'Run' dialog from the Start menu. In Windows Vista, choose **Start > All Programs > Accessories > Run**; in Windows XP, choose **Start > Run**.

6. In the Run dialog, pictured in the next screenshot, delete the text shown in the box, then right-click inside the box and choose **Paste**. The path you copied in step 4 will appear in this box.

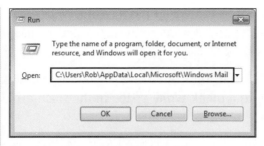

*Paste the path into the **Run** dialog*

7. Click **OK**. The Run dialog will close and a folder window will open.

8. If you're using Outlook Express, this folder contains what you've been looking for, and you can ignore this step. If you use Windows Mail, the window contains a variety of files and folders: find the one named **Local Folders** and double-click it.

9. Now you're looking at the items you need to copy to your new PC. For this I suggest using a USB flash drive (ideally – to avoid any confusion – an empty one). Plug your flash drive into your PC. In Windows Vista, an 'AutoPlay' dialog may appear, so click **Open folder to view files** and a folder window will open showing the contents of your flash drive; in XP, a folder window should open automatically. (In either case, if you don't see this folder window, choose **Computer** or **My Computer** from the Start menu then double-click your flash drive's icon.)

10. Now it's time to copy all those email-related files from the window you were using in step 8 to your flash drive. In that window, start by pressing **Ctrl+A** to select all the items in that folder. You can then copy them to the flash drive using any method you're comfortable with, such as:

• Press **Ctrl+C** to copy the items to the clipboard,

then switch to the flash drive's window, click a blank white space in its right-hand section and press **Ctrl+V**.

- Drag the email files out of their window and drop them on to a blank white space in the flash drive's window.

11. Once the files have been copied to your flash drive, you're done. Close the windows you were using and unplug your flash drive.

That's the first half of the transfer process complete and, you'll be pleased to hear, it was the more complicated part. The remaining job is to connect the flash drive to your new PC and get those email messages on to your new PC. Your new PC may be using Windows Mail, Outlook Express, or the newer Windows Live Mail – the steps are almost identical for each.

After connecting your flash drive to the new PC, if an AutoPlay dialog appears, or a folder window opens, you can close it by clicking the **x** button in its top-right corner as we don't need to use it. Then continue like this:

1. Start the email program on your new PC.

2. When the email program starts, open its **File** menu, move to **Import** and click **Messages**. (If you can't see the **File** menu, press the **Alt** key on your keyboard and it will appear.)

3. Now you'll see a dialog containing a section like the one pictured in the next screenshot, asking which email program you want to 'import' from. The list varies a little depending on which email program you're using on the new PC, but you'll find Windows Mail and Outlook Express among the options: select the program you were using on your old PC, then click **Next** at the

bottom of this dialog. (If you were using Outlook Express and you see a choice of 'Outlook Express' items in this list, choose **Outlook Express 6**. Remember that Microsoft Outlook is not the same program as Outlook Express.)

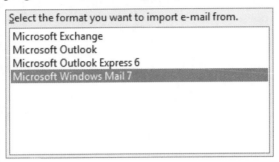

4. If you're importing email from Outlook Express, you may see a dialog with the words 'Specify Location' near the top. If so, select the option **Import mail from an OE6 store directory** and click **OK**.

5. In the next step, click the **Browse** button and a familiar file dialog will appear. In this dialog, you need to locate your flash drive, telling your new email program that this is where it should copy messages from. In Windows 7 or Vista, find and click the **Computer** item in the left panel of the dialog, then double-click your flash drive's icon and click **Select Folder**; in XP, select your flash drive's icon and click **OK**.

6. The box to the left of the **Browse** button you just clicked should now contain the drive letter of your flash drive followed by a colon and a backslash (such as **F:**). Click **Next**.

7. In the next step, make sure there's a blob beside the **All folders** option and click **Next** again.

8. Your new email program will copy your email messages from your flash drive (which should only take a matter of seconds, unless you had thousands of messages), and then you'll see a confirmation that your messages were imported successfully.

9. Click **Finish**, and you're done. You should now find all your email messages in your new email program and you can delete them from your flash drive.

■ How Can I Backup Emails Stored in Microsoft Outlook?

I use Microsoft Outlook for email and I would like to keep a backup copy of the email I receive, but I don't know where the messages are stored. Can you help?

Microsoft Outlook is Microsoft's heavyweight email program, included with some versions of Microsoft Office, and it does quite a lot more than just managing email. Among other things, you can store appointments in its built-in calendar, make notes, and keep track of projects.

Your email messages (along with your appointments, notes and projects) are all stored in a single file, so making a backup (safety) copy is quite straightforward once you know where to find this file. Follow these steps:

1. Start Microsoft Outlook if it isn't already running.

2. In the list of folders at the left of the window, right-click **Personal Folders**. A menu will appear: choose the **Properties** item at the bottom of the menu.

3. In the window that appears, click the **Advanced** button near the bottom.

4. Another window will open, similar to the one pictured in the next screenshot. In the box labelled **Filename** you'll find the name of the file in which Outlook stores all your email messages and other details. Highlight the entire name in this box by swiping over it with the mouse, and then press **Ctrl+C** to copy it to the clipboard.

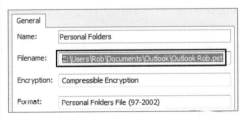

5. Now click **Cancel** in the two windows you opened along the way, and finally close Microsoft Outlook itself.

6. Next, choose **Start > Run** (or press **Win+R**, the Windows flag key and the 'R' key) to open the **Run** command.

7. In the little Run command window, delete any text shown in the box, and then press **Ctrl+V**. The filename you copied in step 4 will appear in this box.

8. Before clicking OK, there's one important thing to do. You need to delete the end of this text, removing every character after the last \ sign in the name. Just before you do this, make a mental note of what that last piece of the name is. In my case, the full text says: C:\Users\Rob\Documents\ Outlook\Outlook Rob.pst so I'll remove the part that says 'Outlook Rob.pst'.

9. Now click **OK**. The folder containing your personal Outlook file will open, and you'll be able to see the name you just noted among the other files it contains. This is your personal Outlook file, and you can now copy it to a backup disk for safety. (Note that this file will be too large to fit on a floppy disk, so you'll have to copy it to a CD, flash drive or external hard disk.)

■ Copy Your Windows XP Address Book to Windows 7/Vista

I've just bought a new Windows 7 computer and copied most of my files to it. My one sticking point is my email Address Book: I can't find out where that is to copy it.

Neither Windows 7 nor Vista has the same Address Book program as Windows XP, so, even if you had found the file, simply copying it to the new PC wouldn't achieve the result you obviously want, which is to make all your contacts' details accessible on the new computer.

Nevertheless, that result is certainly possible to achieve. Just follow these steps:

1. On the Windows XP computer, go to **Start** > **All Programs** > **Accessories** > **Address Book**.

2. When the Address Book window appears, open its **File** menu, move the mouse down to **Export** and click **Address Book (WAB)**.

3. In the dialog that appears next, click the large **Desktop** button in the left-hand panel, type the name **Addresses** in the **File name** box and click **Save**.

4. Almost instantly you'll see a message telling you that your address book has been successfully 'exported'. Click **OK**.

5. Close the Address Book window, and have a look on your desktop where you'll find a new file named 'Addresses'.

6. The next step is to copy this 'Addresses' file to a flash drive or CD so that you can get it to your new PC.

7. Once you've done that, switch to your new PC and plug in the flash drive (or insert the CD) containing this file. However, there's no need to copy that file to the new PC. You just need to be able to see the file it contains, so if necessary go to **Start** > **Computer** and double-click the icon for your flash drive or CD drive.

8. Double-click that **Addresses** file and you'll see the message shown in the next screenshot. Click **Import**.

9. After a few seconds, another dialog will tell you that your contacts have been imported. Click **OK** and you're done. If you open the Start menu, click your name, and then double-click the **Contacts** folder to open it, you'll see a separate 'contact' file for each person in your XP address book.

Microsoft Word Troubleshooting: Create Error Free Stylish Documents with Ease

"I use Word all the time – how can I stop annoying features interrupting my work?"

■ Why Do I Get Several Copies When I Paste Text?

*I was following steps to copy and paste text from one place to another, which involved pressing **Ctrl+C** and **Ctrl+V**. Afterwards, I found I had several copies of the text in a row. Is it me or my computer that's doing it wrong?*

I'm afraid it's probably you! The most likely explanation is that when you press the Ctrl+V key combination to paste the text, you're holding those keys down for longer than you should.

You probably know that if you're typing and you hold a key down for a few seconds, the key repeats automatically, giving you a long string of the same character. Exactly the same thing happens if you press Ctrl+V and keep those keys held down: they repeat automatically, sending numerous 'paste' commands and therefore causing numerous copies of the text to be pasted into your document one after the other.

You may feel tempted to hold down the Ctrl+V keys until you've seen the text appear in your document, and that may be too long. As soon as you press Ctrl+V your PC has to do a little work before the text appears, and it's possible that a second, third or even fourth 'paste' command has been sent while this work is being done, resulting in several copies of the text appearing. This can be quite common on older PCs which process commands more slowly.

The trick is just to tap the **V** key fairly quickly, just as you would if you were typing a letter V. In fact, you can approach it in the same way as typing a capital 'V' (using Shift+V) but using the Ctrl key in place of the Shift key.

■ Why Do I Get an Extra Blank Page When Printing?

Sometimes when I print a document that should be one page long, the printer gives me two pages, but the second is completely blank. Why does this happen?

It shouldn't happen very often, but unless you know the reason, it can be very puzzling when it does. It's not a huge problem of course – you just pop the blank page back into the printer to be used next time – but what causes it?

Quite simply, it's because your document actually is two pages long, but that second page doesn't contain any printable characters, only blank lines. As you know, when you type a document you press the **Enter** key to add a blank line and/or start a new paragraph. If you press **Enter** a few more times, you'll add more blank lines, moving gradually further down the page. Eventually, you'll press Enter once more and you'll be on to a second page. That second page will be sent to your printer, along with the first, when you print the document, but as it doesn't contain any text it will pass straight through the printer with nothing being printed on it.

The way to avoid this is straightforward. When you've finished typing a document and you're ready to print it, press the key combination **Ctrl+End** which makes the cursor jump down to the very last line in your document (whether it's a blank line or not). You'll now see immediately if there are blank lines below the last line you typed, and whether those blanks are numerous enough to have extended your document on to an unnecessary extra page. If they have, press the **Backspace** key repeatedly, removing one blank line with each press, until you've deleted enough blank lines that the unnecessary extra page has been removed.

■ Prevent Accidental Presses of the Insert Key in Microsoft Word

*Every so often when I'm typing in Microsoft Word, I must press the **Insert** key accidentally (perhaps while aiming for the **Delete** key). This has the effect of switching Word into 'Overtype' mode so that, without noticing, everything I type is replacing text I've typed previously. Is there any way to switch off the Insert key to prevent this happening?*

The Insert key causes this problem in almost any word processor and it certainly is annoying. Your keyboard operates in two different typing modes:

- **Insert mode:** This is the normal mode. If you click in the middle of a paragraph of text and start typing, the new text you type is inserted at that position, pushing the text that follows it forward to make room.

- **Overtype mode:** In this mode, when you click in the middle of a paragraph and start typing, the new text you type erases the text that follows it – you're typing over that text, and it gradually disappears.

Each press of the Insert key on your keyboard switches back and forth between these two modes. Unfortunately, it's all too easy to press this key by accident and not notice. Later, you start making changes in the middle of a paragraph you've typed, and when you look up you find that you've just replaced a chunk of perfectly-good text!

In most word processors you can choose **Edit** > **Undo** (or press **Ctrl+Z**) a few times to undo the changes, putting back your lost text, then press the **Insert** key to switch back to Insert mode, and start editing the paragraph again.

Better still, in Microsoft Word, you can prevent this from ever happening at all: just tell Word to ignore that Insert key and never switch to Overtype mode. In Word 2010/2007 this is quick and easy; in earlier versions of Word it takes just a little more effort. Follow the appropriate set of steps below.

Word 2010/2007:

1. In Word 2010, click the **File** tab on the Ribbon followed by **Options**. In Word 2007, click the circular Office button followed by **Word Options**.
2. In the window that appears, click **Advanced** in the panel at the left.
3. Remove the ticks beside **Use the Insert key to control overtype mode** and **Use overtype mode**.
4. Click **OK**.

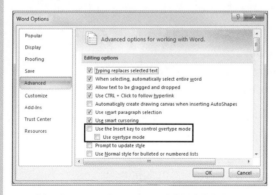

Disable the Insert key in Word 2010/2007

Word 2003/2002/XP:

1. Go to **Tools** > **Macro** and choose **Record New Macro**.

2. You'll see the dialog pictured below. In the topmost box, labelled **Macro name**, type the name **NoInsertKey**.

3. Click the **Keyboard** button.

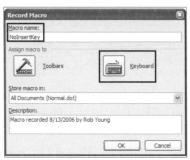

4. Now another dialog will appear, as shown in the next screenshot. Press the **Insert** key on your keyboard. (When you do this you'll see the word 'Insert' appear in the box halfway down on the right.)

5. Click the **Assign** button at the bottom-left of the window, and then click the **Close** button at the bottom-right.

6. Now you'll see the tiny square box pictured below (you may have to hunt around your screen for this, but it usually appears somewhere near the left edge of the Microsoft Word window). In this little box, click the square button on the left.

7. This little box disappears and you've finished. In future, Word will completely ignore the Insert key when you press it, and you'll never find you've accidentally switched to Overtype mode again.

■ How to Hide the Ribbon in Office 2010/2007

I have just made the switch to Microsoft Word 2007 and I'm finding that the Ribbon takes up a lot of space on the screen. Is there a way I can make it smaller?

The 'Ribbon' in the 2010 and 2007 versions of Microsoft Office replaces the multitude of toolbars in earlier Office versions. Along with Word, you'll find the Ribbon in Microsoft Excel, Microsoft PowerPoint, Microsoft Outlook, and other Office programs.

Love it or hate it, you certainly might feel the Ribbon takes up too much space. Fortunately, Microsoft has thought of that. You can't actually make it smaller, but you can do the next best thing, which is to hide it entirely when you're not using it. Here's how:

1. Move the mouse up to the row of tabs at the top of the Ribbon ('Home', 'Insert', 'Page Layout', and so on).

2. Right-click anywhere on that row. The context menu shown in the following screenshot will appear.

3. Choose **Minimize the Ribbon**.

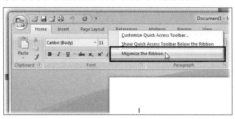

*Right-click any tab and choose **Minimize the Ribbon***

4. As soon as you do this, the Ribbon will vanish, leaving only the row of tabs and allowing you to see more of the document you're working on.

5. Whenever you need to use the Ribbon, just click one of its tabs. The Ribbon will reappear and you can choose the option you want. After you choose an option (or if you click somewhere within your document), the Ribbon will disappear again until the next time you need it.

Click a tab to reveal the Ribbon when you need it

It works exactly the same way in every Office program that has the Ribbon, so you can do this in Excel, PowerPoint and Outlook too if you like to have the Ribbon hidden.

If you decide you're not keen on this 'hide-and-show' Ribbon after all, just follow the first three steps above again, which removes the tick beside the **Minimize the**

Ribbon item and makes the Ribbon permanently visible once more.

■ Move or Copy Text in Word by Dragging It with the Mouse

I discovered by accident that I could move text around in a Microsoft Word document by highlighting it and dragging it to a new position. Is there a similarly easy way to copy some text to a different position?

Dragging text is certainly a quick way to move it around in a Word document. If you've typed a sentence or paragraph in the wrong location, just highlight it, press the left mouse-button somewhere on the highlighted text and drag it to where you want it.

If you want to make a copy of the text somewhere else in the document, you do almost exactly the same thing. The only difference is that you press and hold down the **Ctrl** key before you click-and-drag the text. When you release the mouse button, the text will be copied to the new position instead of being moved there.

Incidentally, this doesn't only work in Microsoft Word; you can use it in Microsoft Works and in the WordPad accessory included with Windows.

■ Word 2010/2007: Automatically Save Documents in the Old Format

I use Microsoft Word 2007, but I try to remember to save all my documents in the old 'Word 97-2003' format so that I can send them to friends who use old versions of Word, and open them on my laptop which has Word XP. I sometimes forget to do this, though, and I wondered if there was a way to make Word save all my documents in this old format automatically?

To briefly clarify the question, all the versions of Microsoft Word from Word 97 to Word 2003 saved their documents in a particular way, and it didn't matter which version of Word anyone used – they would all be able to open one of those documents. However, in Word 2010 and 2007, documents are saved in a different way, and those old versions of Word can't open them. If you use Word 2010/2007, and you need to save a document in such a way that it can be opened in one of those older versions of Word, you have to follow particular steps:

- **Word 2010:** click the blue **File** tab and choose **Save As**. In the dialog that appears, open the drop-down list beside **Save as type** and choose **Word 97-2003 Document**.
- **Word 2007:** click the Office button, move the mouse down to **Save As** and click **Word 97-2003 Document**.

From here, choose where to save the document and type a name for it in the usual way, clicking **Save** to finish.

If, like the questioner, you want to save absolutely every Word document you create in this older format, you don't have to remember to do so; you can tell Word to use this format every time. Here's how:

1. Click the blue **File** tab in Word 2010 and choose **Options**, or click the Office button in Word 2007 and choose **Word Options**.
2. In the window that appears, click **Save** in the left-hand panel.
3. Over to the right, beside 'Save files in this format', open the drop-down list and choose **Word 97-2003 Document (*.doc)**.

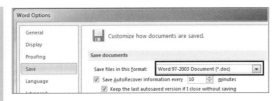

4. Click **OK**.

From now on, whenever you're working on a new document and you're ready to save it, press **Ctrl+S** and the Save As dialog will appear, prompting you for a name. If you look at the 'Save as type' box at the bottom, you'll see that it's already set to 'Word 97-2003 Document' automatically, indicating that the document will be saved in the old format. (Of course, if you want to save this particular document in the new format instead, you can open that box and choose **Word Document** from the top of the list.)

> Exactly the same tip and steps apply to the 2010/2007 versions of other Microsoft Office programs such as Excel and PowerPoint. The Options dialogs of each include the same '97-2003' file format setting in the same place.

■ How Can I Print Using Both Sides of the Paper?

I have a long document to print, and I'd like to be able to print it on both sides of the paper. Apart from printing one page at a time and constantly reinserting sheets into the printer the other way up, I can't see any way to do it. Is there a better way?

There certainly should be a quicker way than that, and by far the best would be to let your printer handle it itself, if it can. Some printers are able to print on both sides of the paper by some clever mechanics (although this may require you to buy an extra gadget, usually known as a 'duplex unit' and attach it to the printer). The manual for your printer should tell you whether two-sided printing is an option, and whether you'll need to buy anything extra to use it.

If your printer can manage two-sided printing, choose **File > Print** in the program you're using, click the **Properties** button to see the options for your printer, and you'll find the corresponding settings in there somewhere. (I can't tell you exactly where, because it will vary from one printer to another, but look out for the word 'Duplex' which is the technical term they may use for it.)

If your printer doesn't do double-sided printing, there's no other choice: you'll have to muck around with pieces of paper yourself! Choose **File > Print** and look at the Print dialog (shown in the next screenshot) to see if there's an option labelled **Manual duplex.** You'll find this option in Microsoft Word and a few other programs, but not many. If you do see this option, you can tick the box beside it and then click **OK** to start printing. After each odd-numbered page has been printed, printing will pause and a dialog will appear on the screen asking you to insert the last sheet of paper again the other way up. Do this and click the button in that dialog to continue printing.

A better alternative is to look for a section marked **Page range** where you can specify which pages of your document to print. In the box labelled **Pages**, type all your odd page numbers separated by commas (such as **1,3,5,7,9**) and click **OK** to print those pages. When the printing is complete, reverse the order of that stack of pages, so that page one is on the bottom, turn the stack the other way up and reinsert it into your printer. Return to the Print dialog and this time type all the even page numbers into the **Pages** box, which prints the even-numbered pages on the reverse of the odd-numbered pages.

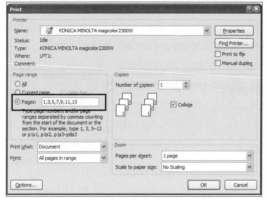

Print odd page numbers first, then print the even-numbered pages on the reverse of those sheets.

Rather than having to enter all the odd and even page numbers yourself, you may find an automatic way to do this. In the print dialog shown in the screenshot, for example, there's a box on the left which currently says **All pages in range**. If you open this box you'll find choices of **Odd pages** and **Even pages**. Simply choose the appropriate option and click **OK** to print.

■ Can I Remove the Margins from a Microsoft Word Document?

I'm trying to design a one-page poster in Microsoft Word and I need to get rid of the enormous margins that Word leaves around the edges of the page. How can I do this?

You probably won't be able to remove the margins entirely: if you were to try, you'd probably find that your printer didn't print the edges of your document. Most printers need to have at least a small margin around the edges of the paper, although it shouldn't have to be as large as the margins Word uses.

Unfortunately, without consulting your printer's manual, it's hard to know what the minimum size of those margins must be. However, there's a trick you can use in Word to make the margins as small as possible:

1. In Word 2010 or 2007, select the **Page Layout** tab on the Ribbon, click the **Margins** button and click **Custom Margins** at the bottom of the menu that appears. In other versions of Word, choose **File > Page Setup**.

2. In the dialog that appears, pictured in the next screenshot, you'll see four boxes showing the current sizes of the top, left, bottom and right margins. To change one of these, just click inside the appropriate box and type a new figure (you don't have to type 'cm' at the end; just a number is enough). Since you want to make all the margins as small as possible, type **0** into all these boxes.

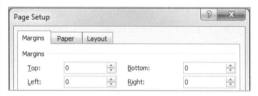

Type 0 as the size for each margin

3. Click **OK** to confirm the changes.

4. If you're lucky, your printer can cope with having no margins at all, but that's unlikely. Instead you'll probably see a message like the one pictured on the next page, which tells you that the margins are too small. Click the **Fix** button.

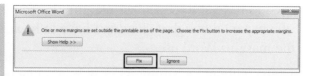

5. Word will return you to the dialog you were just using, and you'll see that the figures in those four boxes have now changed: Word has entered the smallest-possible margin sizes allowed by your printer. (As the next screenshot shows, my printer apparently copes with tiny margins at the top and bottom of the page, and no margins at the sides, but the figures you see will probably differ to some extent.)

6. Without changing these figures (unless you want to increase them), click **OK**. The margins in your document will then be altered to the sizes you've just agreed to, which are as small as they possibly can be.

Master Your Computer with *PC Knowledge for Seniors*

The Complete PC Advice Service Designed Just for You:

✓ Internet, Email and PC Explained without Technical Jargon

✓ Topics Quickly Grasped and Clearly Explained

✓ Free Technical Help for all Your PC problems

With **PC Knowledge for Seniors** you can Master Your PC quickly and easily, from sending email, editing photo's, to solving PC error messages and securing your PC from online threats, you'll have it covered.

We guarantee that the step-by-step advice in PC Knowledge for Seniors covers everything you need to know about your PC and just in case you can't find the answer to your question in the handbook, just email our **FREE technical email advice line** and we guarantee we'll send you the answer within 48 hours.

Request Your Free Trial Today and Discover How To:

- Use 5 expert tips for finding what you want on the Internet quickly and easily
- Stop unwanted spam from reaching your inbox
- Edit your photos like the experts with free photo software
- Secure your PC from online threats with this free highly recommended anti-virus software
- Plus much more...

As a thank you for trying **PC Knowledge for Seniors** on a 6-Week Free Trial we'll also give you **2 Free Bonus Gifts:**

1) **Bonus Gift No 1: Limited Collector's Edition Free CD-ROM** containing anti-virus software, photo editing tools, Microsoft Word letter templates, file compression software and much more...

2) **Bonus Gift No 2: The Bumper Book of PC Technical Terms** – just look up any PC jargon and get the answer fast.

▶ *To claim your 6-week free trial and claim your free gifts fill out the form over the page:*

Agora Business Publications LLP, Nesfield House, Broughton Hall Business Park, Skipton, Yorkshire, BD23 3AN. Registered in England No: OC323533, VAT no: GB 893 3184 95.
Tel: 01756 693180, www.agorabusinesspublications.co.uk

PC Knowledge for Seniors –
6 Week Trial Request Form

❏ YES, I want to learn how to use my computer quickly and easily. And I want to learn how to do it straight away!

Please send me the 450 page **PC Knowledge for Seniors** handbook free-of-charge on a 6 week free trial. If I am convinced by my trial and decide to keep it, I am entitled to take advantage of 33% discount. I will pay just £19.97 instead of the usual price of £29.97. If I decide that it's not for me, I will return it at the end of the trial and owe nothing.

During my Free Trial I have unlimited free access to the PC technical Email Help Service where I can have my problems solved for free.

My FREE CD-ROM and free Book of PC Technical terms are mine to keep whether I decide to pay for the handbook or return it during my 6 week free trial.

If I decide to keep the handbook I don't need to worry about keeping my copy up-to-date - I will automatically be included in the update service. I will be under no obligation to accept these updates (price per page 24p). I will be able to send them back to you upon receipt and this will end my participation in the update service.

Name: _____ Mr / Mrs / Miss / Ms

Address: _____

_____

_____

County: _____

Postcode: _____

PCSB001

100% Risk-Free Guarantee

I will receive **PC Knowledge for Seniors** free of charge and risk-free for a full 6 weeks for review. Within these 6 weeks, I can return the PC Knowledge for Seniors manual at any time and owe nothing. I get to keep the Free Gift CD and PC Book of Technical Terms whatever I decide.

THREE EASY WAYS TO ORDER

SEND BY POST TO:
Agora Business Publications LLP, Nesfield House, Broughton Hall
Business Park, Skipton, Yorkshire, BD23 3AN.

FASTER BY FAX: 01756 693196

OR ORDER ONLINE: www.pcforseniors.co.uk

CUT ALONG DOTTED LINE